Land Law
Law Unit

Land Law
Law Unit

Angela Tannett MA LLB(Cantab), Solicitor
Senior Lecturer, Polytechnic of North London

Anderson Keenan Publishing

First published 1982

Anderson Keenan Publishing Ltd
392 St John Street
London EC1V 4NN

© Angela Tannett 1982

ISBN 0 906501 28 8

Typeset by Columns
Printed and bound in Great Britain by
Spottiswoode Ballantyne Ltd, Colchester.

Contents

General Editor's Preface   vii

Glossary of Key Words   viii

1. **Land**   1
   What is Land? – Why is Land Law so complicated? –
   Limitations on ownership

2. **Estates and Interests**   7
   Legal Estate – Legal Interests – Equitable Interests –
   Position of a Purchaser

3. **Strict Settlements**   13
   Settled Land – How Created – Tenant for Life –
   Trustees – Protection of a Purchaser

4. **Trust for Sale**   19
   How Created – Trustees – Beneficiaries – Protection
   of a Purchaser

5. **Co-Ownership**   27
   Joint Tenancy – Tenancy in Common – Co-ownership and
   Strict Settlement – Determination – Protection of a
   Purchaser

6. **Leases**   35
   Essentials of a Lease – Formalities – Types of Lease –
   Determination – Rights and Obligations – Express
   Covenants – Enforcement of Covenants in Leases –
   Security of Tenure and Rent Restriction

7. **Licences**   51
   Types of Licence – Licences and Leases

8. **Covenants between Freeholders**   59
   Common Law – In Equity – Discharge of Restrictive
   Covenants

9. **Easements**   65
   Essentials – Acquisition of Easements – Special Rules for
   Acquisition of Light – Extent of Easements of Way –

Extinguishment of Easements

10. Mortgages   75
Creation of Mortgages — Mortgagor's Right of Redemption —
Mortgagees Remedies — Protection of Mortgagee against
Subsequent Purchaser or Mortgagees — Discharge of Mortgage

11. Registration   83
Registration of Incumbrances in Unregistered Land —
Registration of Title

12. Contract and Conveyance   97
Precontract — Formation of Contract — Effect of Contract —
Post-contract Conveyancing

Index to Statutes

Index to Cases

General Index

General Editor's Preface

For many years the content of textbooks in law for students taking courses leading to professional qualifications in a variety of fields has been easy to ascertain. Authors have been able to analyse the syllabi of professional bodies and produce in one text chapters covering the various aspects of law required across a wide spectrum so that the student's requirements were met, though in some cases the text went beyond particular needs.

The situation today is very different. Professional bodies are increasingly allowing students to complete various stages of their professional qualifications on the basis of courses in colleges where the syllabus is designed by the lecturers involved who think differently as to topics to be studied and where the examination is set internally by the lecturer to reflect the course.

Thus there is a need for what might be called a 'custom-built' text suitable to a particular approach by a lecturer. Anderson Keenan's Law Units are designed to allow a lecturer, having constructed his course, to recommend a number of suitable Units, as reading for his students so that, by purchasing the relevant Units, the student and lecturer can make up, as it were, a wholly relevant text which covers what the student requires and does not necessitate the purchase of a general text with chapters some of which the student does not require.

In addition the Units are, it is hoped, practical in their approach so that the student for whom law is environmental is not required to study, as a lawyer would, topics which are on the fringe of legal knowledge. This, it is hoped, will tend to more efficient coverage of basic principles, leaving more time to deal with subjects which are fundamental to a particular qualification.

The Units could, it is felt, be extended to areas other than law. In this regard comments of lecturers would be welcome as leading to a further development of the Unit approach.

Denis Keenan

Glossary of Key Words

Land law is often said to be a difficult subject. The words are unusual and the concepts strange. Set out below is a list of some of the most important words and their meanings. When you come across words in the text you feel uncertain about look them up in this list and you will find the topic becomes much clearer.

abstract a summary of the documents showing the title to the property

administrators persons authorised to administer the estate of someone who dies without making a will

assignment a transfer of a reversion of a lease

beneficial owner a person entitled to property for his own benefit and not as a trustee

beneficiary a person entitled under a trust or will

caution an entry protecting an interest in registered land

charge a secured loan

chattels moveable possessions, goods

conditional fee an estate of inheritance given conditionally e.g. to X in fee simple on condition he becomes a surveyor

contractual tenancy a tenancy under a lease or agreement which is still in force

conversion a change either actual or notional in the nature of property e.g. under a trust for sale the interests of the beneficiary are deemed to be in the proceeds of sale

conveyance document transferring property

covenant a promise contained in a deed

covenantee the person entitled to the benefit of the covenant

covenantor the person who makes the promise

curtilage area attached to a dwelling house as part of its enclosure

deed a document under seal

demise a grant of a lease

determine terminate, come to an end

determinable fee an estate of inheritance which will determine on the happening of a certain event, e.g. to X in fee simple until he ceases to practise as a surveyor.

devise a gift of real property by will

dominant tenement land to which the benefit of a right is attached

easement right over land e.g. a right of way

enfranchisement a lessee's right to the freehold under the Leasehold Reform Act, 1967

engrossment a fair copy of a deed or other legal document

equitable interest interest recognised by equity but not by law

equity system of law introduced by the Chancery Courts to mitigate the rigours of the common law

equity of redemption a mortgagor's rights in the mortgaged property

estate the meaning of this word depends on the context. It can mean the length of time an interest in land is held, an area of land, or the property (both real and personal) of a deceased person

estoppel being precluded from a course of conduct by one's own previous behaviour

execute to sign seal and deliver a deed

executors persons appointed by a testator to administer his will

fee simple an estate of inheritance which can be inherited by any class of heirs

fee simple absolute an estate of inheritance which can be inherited by any class of heirs and is not modified (cf. conditional and determinable fees)

fee tail an estate which can only be inherited by lineal descendants i.e. it is a fee which has been cut down

fine a lump sum payment or premium paid on the grant of a lease

fitting a chattel which can be removed from a property

fixture a chattel so fixed to a property that it becomes part of that property

foreclosure proceedings by a mortgagee in a court action which take away the mortgagor's equity of redemption and legal estate

freehold an estate of uncertain duration usually contrasted with leasehold

general equitable charge an equitable charge of a legal estate not protected by title deeds

in gross existing without a dominant tenement

incumbrance a burden on the property

infant a person under 18 years old

intestate a person dying without making a will

joint tenants two or more owners of the legal estate. Also two or more owners of an unsevered equitable interest

leasehold estate granted for a certain duration

letters of administration where a person dies without a will they authorise the administration of the deceased's estate

licence a permission to do something

merger fusion of two or more estates or interests

minor interest interest in registered land which requires to be protected by an entry on the register

mortgage loan secured on property

mortgagor the borrower

mortgagee the lender

overreach transferring interests from land to interests in the purchase money received by the trustees on the sale of the property

overriding interest an interest in registered land which does not appear on the register but which will bind a purchaser whether he knows of it or not

part performance acts done by the plaintiff in reliance on a contract relating to land

periodic letting weekly or monthly letting etc.

personal property money, books, shares etc.

puisne mortgage legal mortgage not protected by deposit of title deeds

real property land and rights over land

regulated tenancy a tenancy protected under the Rent Acts

remainder an interest granted to someone which will vest in the future after a prior interest has come to an end e.g. to A for life with remainder to B

restrictive covenant a covenant restricting the use of land

reversion (1) when a landlord grants a lease he retains a reversion so that when the lease comes to an end he can regain possession of the property

(2) in a freehold estate if a grantor does not part with the fee simple absolute he will retain a reversion e.g. X grants a life interest to A. When A dies X or his estate will have a reversion

root of title a document from which a vendor traces his title

security of tenure protection of a tenant against eviction by his landlord

seisin the possession of land by a freeholder

servient tenement land burdened by a right such as an easement

settlement provision for persons in succession

severance the conversion of a joint tenancy into a tenancy in common

squatter a person in occupation of land adverse to the possession of the documentary owner

statutory owners persons in a strict settlement with the powers of the tenant for life

statutory tenant a Rent Act protected tenant holding over after his contractual tenancy has expired

statutory trusts trusts for sale which arise by statute e.g. where there are joint owners

survivorship the right of a surviving joint tenant to the whole of the deceased tenants' interest

tenancy in common an equitable interest held by co-owners in undivided shares

tenant for life the legal estate owner under a strict settlement

tort civil wrong e.g. trespass or nuisance

trust for sale a trust requiring trustees to sell property

trustee person with fiduciary duties

x

undivided share the interest of a tenant in common

user use or enjoyment

waste acts altering the nature of land; ameliorating (alterations which improve the property) equitable (acts of wanton destruction) permissive (failure to do what ought to be done e.g. repairs) voluntary (doing what ought not to be done e.g. cutting timber)

1 Land

OUTLINE

A. What is land?

1. Physical estate and interests
2. Rights over another's property
3. Fixtures

B. Why is land law so complicated?

1. Permanent Historic growth
2. Economic reasons
   Social reasons
3. Many interests in one piece of land

C. Limitations on Ownership

1. Rights of third party
2. Common law restrictions
3. Statutes e.g. Town and Country Planning Acts

A. WHAT IS LAND?

Land includes the physical earth with the mines and minerals beneath the surface and buildings erected on the surface. It also includes the interest a man may have in that land such as a freehold or leasehold estate.

Rights over a third party's property also count as land. Thus if A has a right of way over B's land on the sale of A's land such right of way will automatically pass to a purchaser.

A phrase used in land law is *quicquid plantatur solo, solo cedit*; whatever is attached to the ground becomes part of it. This not only means buildings, plants and trees growing naturally on the land but also fixtures. Chattels which are attached to the land become fixtures and thus part of the land itself. There are two tests to decide whether a chattel has become a fixture. One is the degree of annexation and the other is the purpose of annexation. The first test gives the *prima facie* answer; if a chattel is securely attached to the land then it is probably a fixture. The second test is decisive. If the chattel is placed on the land so that it can be enjoyed as a chattel then it is not a fixture. On the other hand if it is put on the land for the more convenient use of the land it is a fixture.

LEIGH v. TAYLOR [1902] AC 157

A man put up some valuable tapestries on the wall of his house. He fixed them by tacks to a framework of wood and canvas which he nailed to a wall. He then died. Did the tapestries pass with the land or were they part of his personal estate? *Held* — they were personal property. They had not ceased to be chattels. They were fixed to the walls for better enjoyment of them as chattels.

c.f. *D'Eyncourt* v. *Gregory* (1866) LR Eq 382

Statues, vases, and stone garden furniture standing on their own weight were *held* to be land as they formed part of the design of a landscaped garden.

Sometimes land law is referred to as real property. This is because in the early days of common law if a freeholder was dispossessed he could claim

3

back the property itself, the *res*, by a real action and did not have to accept a monetary compensation. A wrongdoer depriving an owner of personal property could choose and pay damages rather than return the stolen article. Leases were outside the feudal system of landholding. They were regarded as a commercial interest providing an investment for capital. Thus the real action was not available to a dispossessed leaseholder. Today though still technically personal property leases are treated for most purposes as land and are sometimes referred to as chattels real indicating their hybrid nature. Most other systems of law divide more logically into immovables i.e. interests in land, and movables i.e. all other property which would include goods, chattels, stock and shares, rather than into real and personal property.

B. WHY IS LAND LAW SO COMPLICATED?

Land is permanent. Many of the rules were developed originally in feudal times. Although the law has developed to meet the needs of modern society it reflects not a clean sweep but a continuous historical growth through many centuries.

Land being a scarce resource can never remain wholly within the control of private individuals. The need for security and social control of land has resulted in much Rent Act legislation reflecting the often conflicting political thought of the twentieth century. This legislation has been enacted piecemeal and is excessively complicated. Economic factors and the need for allocating land use for the country as a whole has resulted in tax laws affecting land and The Town and Country Planning Acts which superimpose a system of public law on individual rights and obligations.

Even if social, economic and historical factors did not predominate land law would still be complicated because of the many estates and interests both present and future, absolute and limited, which are possible in the same piece of land.

> *Example*: Z settles land on A for life or until he ceases to be a solicitor and then to B absolutely. A charges the property by way of legal mortgage, grants a lease to C, and a right of way over his land is given to D.

C. LIMITATIONS ON OWNERSHIP.

It is sometimes said that 'he who owns the soil owns everything down to the centre of the earth and up to the sky' (*Cuius est solum, eius est usque ad coelum et ad inferos*). This has never been quite true. An estate owner has never been free to use and dispose of land exactly as he wants.

At common law a man is liable in tort for injuries to third parties by his acts or omissions or for causing a nuisance on his land. He cannot claim Treasure trove, i.e., gold and silver hidden in land where the true owner is unknown. Treasure trove belongs to the crown. A landowner cannot own wild animals on his land though he has the exclusive right to kill them and then they fall into his ownership.

Numerous statutes have restricted further the rights of an owner of land. Under The Coal Industry (Nationalisation) Act, 1946, coal is vested in the National Coal Board and under the Petroleum (Production) Act, 1934, oil and natural gas in underground strata belong to the crown. By The Civil Aviation Act, 1949, aeroplanes have the right of passage at a reasonable height over property.

BERNSTEIN v. SKYVIEWS AND GENERAL LTD [1978] QB 749

The defendants were *held* not liable in trespass for flying several hundred feet over the plaintiffs house even though their purpose was to take photographs and sell them to the plaintiffs.

The Water Resources Act, 1963 stipulates that a licence is necessary to abstract water from a source of supply unless the water is used for domestic purposes of the occupier's household or for agricultural purposes other than spray irrigation.

The main Statutory restrictions imposed on the right of a landowner to use his property as he wishes are imposed by the Town and Country Planning legislation. In the 1940's it became apparent that urban development had to be controlled on a nationwide level. The Town and Country Planning Act, 1947 was a result, the first of a series of planning acts. The current legislation is consolidated in the Town and Country Planning Act, 1971 as subsequently amended. The basic effect of the Act is that planning permission must be obtained from the local Planning Authorities when development of property is intended. Development is defined as 'the carrying out of building, engineering, mining or other operations, in, on, over, or under land, or the making of any material change in use of any buildings on the land.' Development does not include, and so permission is not necessary for, interior works not affecting the external appearance of the property, use of land for forest and agriculture, use of land within the curtilage of a house for any purpose incidental to the enjoyment of the house and change of use of the building for the purpose of any class specified in the Town and Country Planning (Uses Class) Order, 1972, to any other purpose in the same class. Certain classes of development specified in the General Development Order, 1977 (or any replacement thereof) do not require permission, e.g. the enlargement of a dwelling house, including a garage, within the curtilage provided it does not exceed 50 cubic metres or one-tenth of the total area subject to a maximum of 115 cubic metres.

2 Estates and Interests

OUTLINE

A. Legal Estate

   1. Fee simple absolute in possession
   2. Term of years absolute

B. Legal Interests

   1. Easements, rights and privileges
   2. Rentcharges
   3. Mortgages
   4. Statutory charges on land
   5. Rights of re-entry

C. Equitable Interests

   1. Equitable interests in a person's own land
   2. Equitable interests over a neighbour's land

D. Position of a Purchaser

   1. He will be bound by legal rights
   2. Family rights under a settlement or trust for sale will be over reached
   3. Most third party equitable rights of a commercial nature will bind him if protected by registration
   4. Equitable rights which are not overreachable or registerable will bind a purchaser who takes with notice of them

A. THE LEGAL ESTATE

Since 1925 there are only two legal estates. The fee simple absolute in possession, commonly called freehold, and the term of years absolute, commonly called leasehold.

An estate indicates how long an interest in land will continue. The fee simple absolute in possession continues almost indefinitely. The word fee indicates that it is an estate of inheritance, and simple that such an estate can be inherited by the heirs generally i.e. it is not limited to a particular class of heirs. Absolute distinguishes the fee from modified fees which today only exist as equitable interests under a trust. Possession includes not only physical possession but receipts of rents and profits. Thus someone can have a fee simple absolute in possession when the whole of the property is let to a tenant.

A term of years absolute, often referred to as a lease, is an estate of fixed duration granted by a landlord to a tenant. It can be either for a fixed term e.g. 10 years, or a periodic tenancy e.g. weekly, monthly or yearly.

B. LEGAL INTERESTS

Section 1 of the Law of Property Act, 1925 provides that there are only five possible legal interests; easements rights or privileges, rentcharges, mortgages, certain statutory charges on land and rights of re-entry.

The most important are easements and mortgages. Easements are rights over land e.g. a right of way. To be legal, such a right must be granted for a length of time equivalent to a fee simple or term of years. Mortgages are charges on real property in favour of someone who has lent money to the legal estate owner.

For an estate or interest to be legal it must come within the category of legal estates or interests in section 1 of the Law of Property Act, 1925. It is not possible for any other interest to be legal. However, because an estate or interest is within the possible legal category this does not mean it *must* be legal. It could be equitable. There are four requirements for an estate or interest to be legal:
1. It must come within s 1 of the Law of Property Act, 1925

2. The proper formalities must be observed. Generally legal estates or interests must be created or transferred by deed.

3. The transferor must have the ability to create or transfer a legal estate or interest e.g. if a mortgagor only has an equitable interest he cannot create a legal mortgage.

4. The estate owner must have the intention to create or transfer a legal estate or interest.

C. EQUITABLE INTERESTS

1. In a person's own land

To be a legal freehold, the estate must be a fee simple absolute in possession. If any of those elements is missing then the freehold interest must be equitable and exist behind a trust for sale or strict settlement.

Thus if it is not a fee, i.e. an estate of inheritance, it must be equitable. A life interest cannot therefore be legal and will take effect as an equitable interest under a strict settlement or trust for sale.

If the fee is not a fee simple i.e. inheritable by the heirs generally but can only be inherited by a restricted class of heirs, it will not be a legal estate. A fee tail is an interest which has been 'cut down' and can only be inherited by lineal descendants.

The fee simple must be absolute if it is to be a legal estate. Thus determinable and conditional fee simples will be equitable interests.

Finally, the fee simple must be in possession to qualify as a legal estate. If the grant is to take effect in the future it will be an equitable interest. Thus a grant to A when he is 25 (A only being 17 at the time of the grant) or to B for life with remainder to C in fee simple must be equitable. Similarly if D grants a life interest to E, on the ending of that interest a fee simple will automatically revert to D's estate. This reversion of the fee simple must be equitable.

A lease for more than three years must be by deed to confer a legal estate. Otherwise such a lease will only amount to an equitable interest.

2. Equitable interests over a neighbour's land

Easements, rentcharges, mortgages and right of re-entry can exist as equitable interests if they are not created formally or if the grantor lacked either the intention or the ability to create a legal interest.

In addition there is a wide range of interests which can only be equitable. These include estate contracts, restrictive covenants and licences, all of which will be dealt with more fully later in the book.

D. POSITION OF A PURCHASER

1. Legal estates and interests are said to bind all the world. Thus a purchaser will be bound by a legal estate or interest whether he knows of it or not.

2. Equitable interests of a family nature which arise under a trust for sale or strict settlement will not bind a purchaser provided he pays the purchase price to at least two trustees. Notice of such interests is irrelevant. The purchaser will take the land free of the interests which will be satisfied out of the purchase money. This is known as overreaching. Thus a purchaser will not be concerned with future interests, determinable fee simples, fee tails or life interests.

3. Commercial equitable interests giving an outsider an interest in the property will bind a purchaser if registered under the Land Charges Act, 1972, or, where the land is registered, protected by an entry on the register under the Land Registration Act, 1925. Thus equitable easements and restrictive covenants should be registered to bind a purchaser. If they are not registered a purchaser will take free of them whether he knows of them or not.

4. There is a residuary class of equitable interests which are not over-reachable or registerable. They will bind a purchaser unless he can prove he is a bona fide purchaser of the legal estate without notice of such interest or a person claiming through such a purchaser. Notice may be actual or constructive. It is constructive where there was notice of some incumbrance and a proper enquiry would have revealed what it was, or where a purchaser deliberately abstains from making an enquiry or does not make an enquiry due to carelessness or some other reason. A purchaser should check up on a vendor's title in unregistered land for at least the past fifteen years and should inspect the land to see if there are any occupiers claiming rights. If a solicitor or other agent receives notice in that particular transaction it will be imputed to the purchaser. Two examples of equitable interests which bind a purchaser with notice are equitable rights of re-entry and licences arising by estoppel.

UNREGISTERED LAND

LEGAL

EQUITABLE

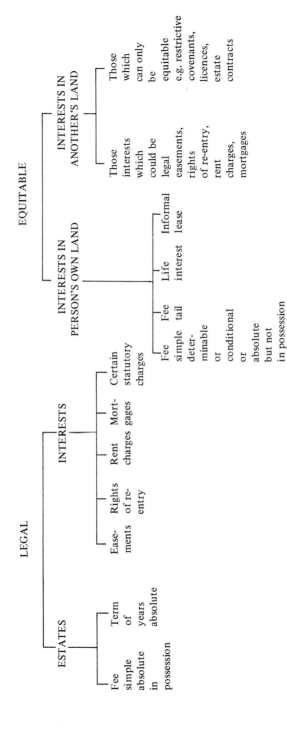

ESTATES

Fee simple absolute in possession

Term of years absolute

INTERESTS

Easements

Rights of re-entry

Rent charges

Mortgages

Certain statutory charges

INTERESTS IN PERSON'S OWN LAND

Fee simple determinable or conditional or absolute but not in possession

Fee tail

Life interest

Informal lease

INTERESTS IN ANOTHER'S LAND

Those interests which could be legal e.g. easements, rights of re-entry, rent charges, mortgages

Those which can only be equitable e.g. restrictive covenants, licences, estate contracts

3 Strict Settlements

OUTLINE

A. Settled Land Arises Where Land Is:

1. Limited to persons by way of succession
2. Granted to an infant
3. Subject to a family charge

B. How Created

1. Trust Instrument
2. Vesting Deed

C. Tenant For Life

1. Legal Estate vested in him
2. His powers
3. Safeguards against abuse

D. The Trustees

1. General supervisory powers
2. How ascertained

E. Protection Of A Purchaser

1. Where imperfect settlement
2. Where settlement correctly created
3. Overreaching
4. Termination of settlement

INTRODUCTION

A settlement is a disposition of real or personal property made either by will or deed which sets up a series of interests in favour of a succession of persons.

Strict settlements were popular in the days when the upper classes had landed estates which they wanted to preserve for future generations. Today settlors are more likely to settle property by means of a trust for sale unless they wish to vest the control of the property and the power of sale in the principal beneficiary. However strict settlements are sometimes created by mistake where a testator in a home-made will leaves property to his wife for life with remainder to his children. A strict settlement is governed by the Settled Land Act, 1925.

A. SETTLED LAND ARISES WHERE LAND IS:

1. limited to persons by way of succession, e.g. to A for life with remainder to B for life with remainder to C in fee simple. It would also include
   (a) an entailed interest, e.g. to A in tail with a reversion to the grantor;
   (b) a gift to A in fee simple with a gift over on the happening of a certain event;
   (c) a determinable fee simple, e.g. to A in fee simple until he ceases to practise as a solicitor;
   (d) a conditional fee simple, e.g. to A in fee simple on condition that he resides in the property and provides a house for X there. If the condition is broken then the property should go to B; and
   (e) a gift contingent on the happening of a certain event, e.g. G grants land to A and B on trust for X in fee simple if he should reach the age of 35.
2. conveyed to an infant either in fee simple or for a term of years absolute. As an infant cannot hold the legal estate the conveyance operates as an agreement for valuable consideration to execute a settlement and in the meantime to hold the land on trust for the infant.
3. subject to a charge, voluntary or in consideration of marriage, or by any family arrangement with the payment of any sums for the benefit of any person, e.g. to X in fee simple subject to an annuity of £100 in favour of Y.

15

B. HOW CREATED

Two documents are needed to create a strict settlement. The trust instrument declares the trusts on which the land is to be held and appoints the trustees. If the settlement is created by will then the will is the trust instrument. Generally the trust instrument will not concern the purchaser. It is said to be 'behind the curtain'. The document which concerns the purchaser is the vesting deed. This conveys the legal estate to the tenant for life or declares that he has a legal estate.

If the settlement is set up by one document only then the legal estate remains in the settlor. The one document operates as the trust instrument and the tenant for life can request the trustees to execute a deed in his favour. It is the trustees and not the settlor who must execute the deed. If there are no trustees and no person willing and able to appoint them, than an application must be made to the court for the appointment of trustees. Until a second document has been executed by the trustees no disposition of the legal estate can be made.

C. THE TENANT FOR LIFE

The vesting deed (or vesting assent where the trust instrument is a will) vests the legal estate in the tenant for life. He has two interests; his own equitable life interest and the entire legal estate which he holds for himself and the other beneficiaries of the settlement. The tenant for life is generally the beneficiary of full age who is entitled to the first interest in possession under the settlement. He is 'the man on the spot' who will be most involved in the management of the property. If the tenant for life is an infant or there is no tenant for life (e.g. where the first life interest is not to begin until a future marriage), the legal estate will be vested in the statutory owners. The statutory owners are any persons on whom the settlement expressly confers the powers of a tenant for life or otherwise the trustees of the settlement.

The policy of the Settled Land Act, 1925 is that the person vested with the legal estate, who is normally the tenant for life, should be empowered to deal with the land in much the same way as a fee simple owner. However, any gain arising out of the exercise of this power is to be held on trust by the tenant for life for the beneficiaries according to the terms of the settlement.

The powers of the tenant for life include the power to sell, lease, mortgage the legal estate, grant an option, effect improvements and select investments. These powers cannot be given to anyone other than the tenant for life or statutory owner. Any attempt to fetter these powers is void. Additional powers can be given to the tenant for life either under the terms of the settlement or by order of the court.

Because the tenant for life has such extensive powers it is important that he should not abuse them. He is a trustee of such powers which he must exercise not only for his own ends but for the benefit of the whole settlement. Generally, the tenant for life does not need the consent of the trustees before exercising his powers but he has to give them notice of his intention to do so. Section 18 of the Settled Land Act provides that any capital money has to be paid not to the tenant for life but to the trustees of the settlement. If a purchaser does not comply with this requirement, he will not obtain the legal estate. The same section provides that any disposition not authorised by the Settled Land Act will be void.

As the tenant for life has only a limited interest in the property he must preserve its value for his successors. Thus he will be liable for waste if he spoils or destroys the land or buildings.

D. THE TRUSTEES

The function of the trustees is to exercise a general supervision of the settlement and in particular to receive any capital money on a sale. The trustees will normally be specifically nominated by the settlor in the deed of settlement. If the settlement is created by will, in default of other people being appointed, the personal representatives of the settlor will act as trustees.

E. PROTECTION OF A PURCHASER

1. Where a settlement has only been created by one document a purchaser who has no knowledge of a tenant for life being entitled to a vesting deed will obtain a good title from the legal estate owner.
2. Where there has been a properly constituted settlement, a purchaser in good faith will be deemed to have complied with all the requirements of the Act. Thus to some extent the rigours of s 18 are mitigated by s 110(i) of the Settled Land Act.

RE MORGAN'S LEASE [1972] Ch. 1

In 1960 the tenant for life by a document not under seal granted a lease of seven years, with an option to renew. In 1962 the tenant for life died and the legal estate was vested in the defendant on trust for sale. In 1967 the lessee gave notice that he wanted to exercise his option. D did not want him to do so and claimed that the lease was invalid because it was not at the best possible rent and was not by deed. *Held* that the lessee was protected by s 110(i) as he had acted in good faith and thus was entitled to exercise the option.

3. If a purchaser pays the capital money to two trustees he will not be

concerned with the equitable interests arising under the settlement. These interests are 'overreached', that is transferred from interests in land to interests in purchase money.

4. When a strict settlement comes to an end the trustees should execute a deed of discharge. This would entitle a purchaser to assume that the settlement had ended. Even without such a deed if a conveyance or assent relating to land which was formerly settled does not refer to trustees of the settlement, the purchaser must assume that the person in whom the deed vests the property is absolutely entitled free of all interests under the settlement (s 110(5)).

4 Trust for Sale

OUTLINE

A. How Created

    1. By one or two documents
    2. Automatically in the case of co-ownership

B. Trustees

    1. Legal estate vested in trustees
    2. Their powers
    3. Safeguards against abuse

C. Beneficiaries

    1. Delegation of powers to them of leasing and management
    2. Consents
    3. Consultation

D. Protection of a Purchaser

    1. Overreaching
    2. Purchaser not concerned with consultation or more than two consents
    3. Can assume trust for sale is subsisting

INTRODUCTION

A trust for sale can be created expressly e.g. a conveyance to T1 and T2 to hold on trust for sale for A for life with remainder to B in fee simple, or to T1 and T2 to hold on trust for sale for A and B jointly.

T1	T2		—	Legal Estate
A for life	B remainder in fee simple		—	Equitable interest

OR

T1	and	T2	—	Legal Estate
A		B	—	Equitable concurrent interest.

The first example is similar to a succession of interests set up by a strict settlement. Heavy taxes makes it generally inadvisable to set up trusts of this kind whether by way of strict settlement or trust for sale. The main exception is where a life interest is given to a spouse.

The express trust for sale to give effect to concurrent interests is frequently used. Often the trustees will be the same people as the beneficiaries.

In certain circumstances a statutory or implied trust for sale will arise. The main examples are where land is owned concurrently by two or more owners or where a person dies intestate i.e. without making a will.

A. HOW CREATED

In order for there to be a trust for sale there must be a duty to sell, not a mere power. Either the word 'trust for sale' must be used or the document must be carefully construed to see if it contains a trust for sale or not. A trust either to retain or sell the land is construed as a trust to sell with the power to postpone the sale. When deciding whether a document creates a strict settlement or a trust for sale the first question to ask is: Is there an immediate binding trust for sale? 'Immediate' means that the trust to sell must not arise in the future e.g. to T on trust for sale when X reaches 21 would not be a trust for sale but a strict settlement. It can still be a trust for sale even if the consent of a third party is needed before the trustees can sell the property. The meaning of the word 'binding' is uncertain.

A trust for sale can be created by one document. When complicated trusts are set up or property is left by will then there will be two documents, a trust instrument declaring the trusts and a document conveying the legal estate. A purchaser will only be concerned with the second document.

B. TRUSTEES

The legal estate is vested in the trustees. They have all the powers which the tenant for life and trustees have under a strict settlement. However the exercise of the trustees' power of sale may be made subject to the consents of specified beneficiaries. Thus a settlor may be able to ensure that property is not sold but retained in the family more successfully by a trust for sale than by a strict settlement. A tenant for life's power of sale cannot be restricted in any way.

The Law of Property Act, 1925 gives the trustees power to postpone the sale except where the trust provides to the contrary e.g. a direction to sell the property 'as soon as possible after my death' would mean that the trustees could not postpone the sale. In order to postpone a sale the trustees must be unanimous. If only one of three trustees wishes to sell then his will must prevail. However where a trustee refuses to act any interested party may apply to the court under s 30 of the Law of Property Act. The court may find that notwithstanding the duty to sell there is a collateral object of the trust to preserve the land which will take precedence over the trust for sale.

JONES v. CHALLENGER [1961] 1 QB 176

A married couple purchased a leasehold house as the matrimonial home. They provided the money equally and held the lease as joint tenants. Challenger divorced his wife and she married Jones. She applied for an order for sale under s 30. *Held*: that the purpose of the joint tenancy was to provide a matrimonial home so that a sale insisted upon by one of the parties while the marriage was subsisting would defeat the collateral object of the trust for sale. However here the marriage was at an end so that collateral purpose no longer existed and the main duty to sell was restored.

RE BUCHANAN-WOLLASTON'S CONVEYANCE [1939] Ch 738

In 1928 four people were the owners of homes adjacent to a piece of open land. They bought the land providing the money in unequal shares and it was conveyed to them as legal joint tenants. They subsequently entered into a deed reciting that they had purchased the land to ensure that it would not become a nuisance or cause a depreciation in the value of their houses. In 1938 one joint tenant having sold his house wanted to sell the land against the wishes of the others. He applied to the court for the sale of the property. *Held*: that there was a statutory trust for sale but that the court would not compel a sale at the instigation of a person whose object was to avoid his contractual obligations while the underlying purpose of the trust for sale subsisted.

C. BENEFICIARIES

Beneficiaries have none of the powers of a tenant for life under the Settled Land Act. The powers of leasing and management but not of sale may be delegated to a beneficiary of full age beneficially entitled in possession to the rents and profits of the land. Though such a beneficiary will often be in physical possession of the property the traditional view is that a beneficiary has no right to such possession. It is in the discretion of the trustees whether or not to grant the right of occupation. Recent cases have thrown doubt on this view.

As we have seen a beneficiary may have some negative control over the sale of the property. The settlor may have specified that the consent of one or more beneficiaries is necessary for the sale of the property.

In the case of a statutory trust for sale the trustees are bound, where practicable, to consult the full-age beneficiaries in possession and give effect to their wishes so far as is consistant with the general interest of the trust.

D. PROTECTION OF THE PURCHASER

Where on a conveyance by trustees for sale a purchaser pays capital money to two trustees he will take free of the equitable interests under the trust. There is no power under a trust for sale to 'overreach' legal interests nor equitable interests existing when the trust for sale was created. Technically the interests under a trust for sale are regarded as interests in the proceeds of sale from the outset i.e. as soon as the trust is set up and not just at the time of the sale. This is known as the doctrine of conversion. Interests under a trust for sale are said to be interests in personal property not interests in land.

RE KEMPTHORN [1930] 1 Ch 268

T owned a share in a freehold house under a trust for sale. He died leaving by his will all his real property to F and all his personal property to P. P not F obtained the interest in the house because being land subject to a trust for sale it was treated not as land but as personal property.

23

The courts however have not been consistent in their application of the doctrine of conversion.

A purchaser is not concerned to see whether or not the trustees have consulted the beneficiaries about the proposed sale nor is he concerned with any direction in a trust instrument about postponing the sale. If the sale requires the consents of certain people, the consent of any two will be sufficient for the purchaser. Thus if the trust requires the consent of three people to the sale and only two are obtained the purchaser will obtain a good title though the beneficiaries will be able to sue the trustees for breach of trust. A purchaser can assume that a trust for sale is continuing (with the result that he will be protected under the provisions of the Act) until it has been conveyed to or under the direction of the persons interested in the proceeds of sale.

COMPARISON CHART SHOWING DIFFERENCES BETWEEN

A Settlements Settled Land Act, 1925	B Trusts for sale Law of Property Act, 1925
1. Legal estate in tenant for life or statutory owners.	1. Legal estate vested in trustees.
2. Tenant for life's powers cannot be fettered.	2. Trustees' powers of sale may be subject to consents of specified persons.
3. Favours one beneficiary, the tenant for life.	3. Beneficiaries can be provided for equally.
4. Advantages: — Control is given to the tenant for life. — Deed of Discharge and presumption of s 110(5) protects a purchaser when settlement at an end.	4. Disadvantages: — Beneficiaries do not have control. The power of sale cannot be delegated. — Purchaser must always insist on two trustees being appointed or investigate the equitable interests to discover if the vendor is absolutely entitled when a trust for sale ends.

5. Disadvantages:
- Expensive; 2 documents needed to set up settlement.

- Special grants of probate needed on death of tenant for life when settlement

5. Advantages:
- Cheaper and simpler.
- No change of legal ownership on death of beneficiary.
- Advantages of strict settlement can be obtained by trust for sale
  (i) power to postpone sale
  (ii) power to delegate leasing and management.

Additional Advantages:
(i) trusts for sale can dispose of a person's entire estate, stocks, shares, money etc. as well as land.
(ii) It is a better way of keeping property in the family. The settlor may specify that the consent of beneficiaries should be obtained before a sale. Alternatively the court might find there was a collateral purpose of the trust and thus not order a sale.

5 Co-Ownership

OUTLINE

A. Joint Tenancy

1. Since 1925 a legal estate must be held by co-owners as joint tenants of which there cannot be more than four.
2. Equitable interests will be held as joint tenants if:
   (a) the four unities are present
   (b) no words of severance are used
   (c) equitable presumptions do not apply.
3. Consequences
   (a) right of survivorship
   (b) legal joint tenancy cannot be severed
   (c) equitable joint tenancy can be severed by:
      (i) acquisition of larger estate than co-tenants'
      (ii) alienation *inter vivos*
      (iii) mutual agreement
      (iv) course of dealing
      (v) notice in writing.

B. Tenancy in Common

1. Since 1925 can only exist as an equitable interest.
2. Arises where
   (a) words of severance are used or
   (b) four unities not present or
   (c) equitable presumptions apply or
   (d) beneficial joint tenancy has been severed.

C. Co-ownership and Strict Settlements

1. Joint tenants together constitute the tenant for life.
2. Where tenants in common hold land it ceases to be settled and becomes subject to a trust for sale.

D. Determination

1. Equitable joint tenancy by severance

2. All forms of co-ownership by:
   (a) partition
   (b) sale
   (c) union
   (d) release.

E. Protection of a Purchaser

1. If he pays capital money to two trustees he will take free of the equitable interests.
2. If a sole surviving trustee states he is beneficially entitled a purchaser will obtain a good title under the Law of Property (Joint Tenants) Act, 1964, provided:
   (a) no bankruptcy petition registered
   (b) no notice of severance
   (c) it is not registered land.
3. If one trustee and a purchaser is a bona fide purchaser of the legal estate without notice he will take free of the equitable interests.

INTRODUCTION

Co-ownership arises where two or more people are entitled to land concurrently. A common example is where a husband and wife own the matrimonial home. Sometimes property is vested in a trust corporation who will hold property on behalf of the investors. They will have an equitable interest as tenants in common in proportion to their investments.

A. JOINT TENANCY

The word tenancy has nothing to do with leaseholds. It simply means ownership. A lease, like any estate or interest, can be co-owned. Since 1925 the legal estate must be held as joint tenants and there cannot be more than four. The equitable interest can be held either as joint tenants or tenants in common.

When does an equitable joint tenancy arise?

In a joint tenancy the four unities must exist, there must be no words of severance and the equitable presumptions must not apply.

(a) The four unities

(i) **The unity of possession.** The possession of the whole land must be vested in each joint tenant. Each of the joint tenants has a right to go onto the land as he wishes and cannot be excluded. Therefore an action for trespass against a co-owner cannot be brought by another co-owner, nor can rent normally be demanded by a non-occupying co-owner from a co-owner in possession.

(ii) **The unity of interest.** The interest of each joint tenant must be the same in extent, nature and duration. If X has a leasehold interest and Y a life interest there can be no joint tenancy.

(iii) **The unity of title.** The title of all co-owners must have been derived from the same act or document.

(iv) **The unity of time.** The title must have vested in the joint tenants at the same time. Thus a gift to A and B in fee simple when each attains the age of twenty-one and A is older than B could not be a joint tenancy.

(b) No words of severance

If words of severance are used then there will be a tenancy in common: e.g.
share and share alike
to be divided amongst
equally
between
So a grant to A and B in fee simple would result in a joint tenancy but to A and B equally would result in a tenancy in common because words of severance have been used.

(c) Equitable presumptions

Equity prefers a tenancy in common because of the unfairness of the doctrine of survivorship. In certain circumstances equity will say there is a tenancy in common.

  (i)   Where the purchase price is paid in unequal shares, e.g. a conveyance to A and B in fee simple where A has paid one-third and B two-thirds of the purchase price. A and B are legal joint tenants but equitable tenants in common as to one-third and two-thirds respectively.

 (ii)   Where two or more persons lend money on a mortgage whether in equal or unequal shares.

(iii)   Where two or more persons purchase land for purposes of business or some other enterprise aimed at making a profit.

Consequences

(a) When one joint tenant dies his interest automatically passes to the other joint tenants and this process will continue until there is only one survivor who then holds the land as sole owner. The right of the survivor prevails over any disposition made by a joint owner's will. If joint owners die together and it is not known who died first then, subject to an order of the court, the younger is presumed to have survived the elder.

(b) A legal joint tenancy cannot be severed.

(c) An equitable joint tenancy can be severed and turned into a tenancy in common. This will destroy the right of survivorship. No joint tenant has a distinct share in the land but he has a potential share equal in size to that of his co-owners. As a result of the severance the co-owner can for the first time say he holds a share in the property. This share is only a mathematical one for even in a tenancy in common there is unity of possession. It is sometimes called a tenancy in undivided shares. The size of the share which a severing tenant will own depends on the number of co-owners, e.g. if he is one of three he will own a third. An equitable joint tenancy can be severed by:

(i)   Acquisition by one tenant of a greater interest than that of his co-tenants. It will not prevent a joint tenancy from arising if one joint tenant was originally given some further estate in the land; land to A, B and C as joint tenants for life with remainder to C in fee simple will not destroy C's joint tenancy for life. The subsequent addition of an estate in land would destroy the unity of interest and sever the joint tenancy, e.g. to A, B and C as joint tenants for life with remainder to C in fee simple and A acquires C's fee simple. This would destroy A's joint tenancy for life.

(ii) Alienation *inter vivos* by one tenant of his potential share to a third party. This severs his joint tenancy and a new owner takes his share as tenant in common; e.g. A, B and C are joint tenants and A sells to X. X is a tenant in common of a third and B and C are joint tenants of two-thirds. All have rights to occupy the land and if B dies then C is a tenant in common of two-thirds. Partial alienation also severs; e.g. the creation by a joint tenant of a mortgage or life interest out of his share.

(iii) Mutual agreement. The equitable joint tenants may contract to sever the joint tenancy.

(iv) By a course of dealings between the parties:

BURGESS v. RAWNSLEY [1975] Ch 429

H and R met at a scripture rally in Trafalgar Square. H was minded to marry R and persuaded R to join in the purchase of the reversion of the house in which H was living. They provided the money in equal shares and the property was conveyed to them as joint tenants. R made it clear that she was not minded to marry H. Negotiations took place for H to buy her interest. An agreement was reached but R subsequently asked for a higher price. H then died. R claimed that because of the doctrine of survivorship she was entitled to the whole house as surviving joint tenant. The Court of Appeal *held* that H had severed the beneficial joint tenancy either by agreement or by a course of dealings and thus H's estate was entitled to a half share in the house.

(v)   By notice in writing under s 36(2) of the Law of Property Act, 1925. The notice has to be communicated to the other co-owners and only applies where the trustees and the beneficiaries are the same people.

B. TENANCY IN COMMON

A tenancy in common can only exist as an equitable interest.

How does it arise?

It arises where
(a) words of severance are used or
(b) the four unities are not present or
(c) the equitable presumptions apply or
(d) a beneficial joint tenancy has been severed.

    An example of (a) is where property is conveyed to A, B and C each as to one third share. An example of (c) is a conveyance to A and B or to A alone where A and B make unequal contributions to the purchase price.

> ### BULL v. BULL [1955] 1 QB 234
>
> The plaintiff and his mother purchased a house for himself and his mother to live in. The house was conveyed in his name alone and the purchase money was provided in unequal shares. The son married and disputes arose between his mother and wife. He sued for possession. The mother was *held* to be an equitable tenant in common and until the house was sold each was entitled to possession and neither could turn the other out.

C. CO-OWNERSHIP AND STRICT SETTLEMENTS

1. Joint tenants.

S 19(2) of the Settled Land Act, 1925 provides that where two or more persons of full age are entitled as joint tenants they together will constitute the tenant for life.
e.g. To A for life, remainder to B and C for life, remainder to D in fee simple. A dies and the legal estate devolves on the Settled Land Act Trustees. As A's special personal representatives they will sign a vesting assent in favour of B and C as joint tenants for life.

2. Tenants in common

If persons entitled to settled land hold as tenants in common the land ceases to be settled land and becomes subject to a trust for sale. The former Settled Land Act trustees can call for the legal estate, if it is not already vested in them and they will then hold it on trust for sale for the beneficiaries as tenants in common. S 36 (1) Settled Land Act, 1925.

D. DETERMINATION

An equitable joint tenancy will come to an end if there is an act of severance. It will then be an equitable tenancy in common.

Joint tenants and tenants in common can partition their land and thus by destroying the unity of possession bring their co-ownership to an end.

If one of two joint tenants dies the survivor will become absolutely entitled. Similarly if one of two joint tenants buys the other's share or releases his interest to the other, co-ownership will end by union in a sole tenant.

E. PROTECTION OF A PURCHASER

1. If a purchaser pays the capital money to two trustees, the equitable interests under the trust will be overreached. This means that they will not concern a purchaser whether he knows of them or not. The beneficiaries' interests will be satisfied out of the purchase money.
2. If the vendor is a sole surviving joint tenant absolutely entitled in law and equity the purchaser will obtain a good title under the provisions of the Law of Property (Joint Tenants) Act, 1964. The vendor must convey as beneficial owner or state in the conveyance that he is absolutely entitled. There must be no receiving order or bankruptcy petition registered as a land charge against any of the joint tenants and no memorandum of severance of the beneficial joint tenancy. The Act does not apply to registered land.
3. If the legal estate was vested in a sole legal owner at the outset then if the purchaser is a bona fide purchaser of the legal estate without notice of the trust he will take free of the equitable interests.

CAUNCE v. CAUNCE [1969] 1 WLR 286

A husband (H) and wife (W) purchased a house providing the purchase money in unequal shares. The legal estate was vested in H's name alone. H was therefore holding the legal estate on trust for sale for himself and W as tenants in common. H, unknown to W, charged the property to the Bank. The Bank was *held* to have no knowledge of W's interest and thus when H went bankrupt it had priority over her interest.

Problem illustrating co-ownership

A, B, C & D buy a house providing a quarter of the purchase money each. A gives written notice to B, C & D that he wishes to sever his interest. B sells his interest to X. A, B, & C are killed in a car crash. Advise D.

Answer:

It is essential in answering this problem to keep the legal estate and equitable interests separate.

Legal estate	*Equitable interest*
1. A, B, C & D joint tenants on purchase	A, B, C, & D joint tenants on purchase
2. A, B, C, & D remain joint tenants when A gives written notice.	A becomes tenant in common of ¼ while B, C, & D remain joint tenants of ¾.
3. A, B, C, & D remain joint tenants when B sells his equitable interest to X	A remains tenant in common of ¼, X becomes tenant in common of ¼ and C & D remain joint tenants of the other half.
4. D becomes sole tenant of the legal estate by survivorship. In order to sell the property he should appoint another Trustee so that the equitable interests will be overreached.	X, A's estate and D are now tenants in common in the shares ¼, ¼ and ½ respectively. D has acquired C's half by survivorship.

6 Leases

OUTLINE

A. Essentials of a Lease

1. Exclusive possession
2. The intention to create the relationship of landlord and tenant
3. Certainty of commencement and term

B. Formalities

1. Legal lease – deed
2. Equitable lease – writing or part performance

C. Types of Lease

1. Fixed term
2. Periodic tenancy
3. Tenancy at will
4. Tenancy at sufferance
5. Leases for lives at a rent
6. Perpetually renewable leases

D. Determination

1. Effluxion of time
2. Notice
3. Surrender
4. Merger
5. Forfeiture

E. Rights and Obligations

1. Landlord
2. Tenant

F. Express Covenants

G. Enforcement of Covenants in Lease

1. Privity of contract
2. Privity of estate

35

3. Indemnity
   — express
   — implied
   — Moule v Garrett (1872) LR 7 Ex 101

4. Position of Landlord

H. Security of Tenure and Rent Restriction

1. Agricultural holdings
2. Business tenancies
3. Residential tenancies
4. Leasehold Reform Act, 1967

INTRODUCTION

It is important to understand the terminology of leases. The diagram below illustrates the parties to a grant and an assignment of a lease.

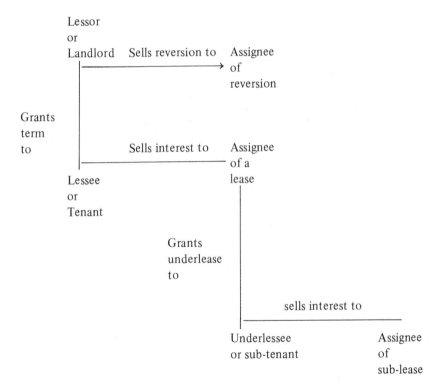

The assignee takes the whole interest and the same term as the assignor. An underlessee takes a shorter term than the original lessee.

A. ESSENTIALS OF A LEASE

There must be:

1. A right to exclusive possession of the property
2. An intention to create the relationship of landlord and tenant.
3. The length and commencement of the term must be certain.

B. FORMALITIES FOR CREATING A LEASE

1. To create a legal estate the lease must be by deed, unless it is for a term not exceeding three years, takes effect in possession and is for the best rent reasonably obtainable without taking a fine. A fine is a premium or capital payment.
2. A contract for a lease for however short a term must be evidenced by writing to comply with section 40 of the Law of Property Act, 1925. As this section is so important it is set out below. It should be noted that it is relevant to all contracts relating to land e.g., vendor and purchaser agreements.

   S 40(1) No action may be brought upon any contract for the sale or other disposition of land or any interest in land, unless the agreement upon which such action is brought, or some note or memorandum thereof, is in writing, and signed by the party to be charged or by some other person thereunto by him lawfully authorised.

   (2) This section applies to contracts whether made before or after the commencement of this Act and does not affect the law relating to part performance or sales by the court.
3. A lease not created by deed can create a valid equitable lease provided it is in writing or is supported by an act of part performance (see p. 99). It will be treated as an agreement to grant a lease by deed.

Equitable leases and agreement for leases should be registered as an estate contract under the Land Charges Act, 1972 if they are to bind a purchaser of the reversion.

C. TYPES OF LEASE

The term lease is usually applied to a fixed term and tenancy to a periodic letting which continues indefinitely until terminated by notice.

1. Fixed term

The length of the term has to be agreed before the lease takes effect. It is still a fixed term even if the lease is capable of being determined before the full period expires. A lease granted after 1925 at a rent is void if it is to start more than 21 years after its creation. Similarly a contract to grant such a lease is void. At common law a fixed term ends on the expiration of the term without the need to give notice. However, today there are wide statutory exceptions.

2. Periodic Tenancy

a) Yearly tenancy

This may be created expressly or it may arise by implication from possession of land and payment of money measured by reference to a year. Subject to contrary agreement, half a year's notice expiring at the end of a completed year of the tenancy is needed to end a yearly tenancy (182 days) or, where the tenancy began on a quarter day (which is the usual agreement), two quarters. The quarter days are 25th March, 24th June, 29th September and 25th December. These are easy to remember because there are 5 letters in March (25th), 4 in June (24th), 9 in September (29th) and no one forgets Christmas day.

b) Monthly or weekly tenancies

These need a whole period of notice, either a week or a month, subject to contrary agreement. If the property let is a dwelling house, even if it is only a weekly tenancy, the Protection from Eviction Act, 1977 provides that four weeks' notice must be given.

3. Tenancy at will

These arise where a landlord agrees to a tenant occupying the land on terms that either party may terminate the agreement at any time. Acceptance of rent on a regular basis may convert the arrangement into a periodic letting.

4. Tenancy at sufferance

These arise when a tenant holds over after the expiry of a lease without the landlord's consent.

5. Leases for lives at a rent

Section 149(6) of the Law of Property Act converts leases for lives or determinable on the marriage of a lessee into terms of ninety years. This section only applies where the leases are granted at a rent or in consideration of a fine. Otherwise they would be life interests under a strict settlement.

6. Perpetually renewable lease

The 1925 Law of Property Act converts perpetually renewable leases into terms of two thousand years, determinable by the lessee only on giving 10 days' notice expiring on one of the old renewal dates. Every assignment of the lease has to be registered with the landlord within six months and the tenant who assigns his lease is not liable for breaches of covenant committed after the assignment. Perpetually renewable leases are often created inadvertently e.g. L. gives T a lease for 3 years with an option to renew on identical terms, including the option to renew for a further term. The courts are astute to find, where possible, an intention that the lease should not be perpetually renewable.

D. TERMINATION OF LEASES

A lease may come to an end by:

1. Effluxion of time

A fixed term will come to an end at the end of the term subject to any statutory extension.

2. Notice

A periodic term will come to an end on expiry of the appropriate notice subject to any statutory protection.

3. Surrender

A tenant may give up an interest in the land. Generally this must be done by deed but it may occur by operation of law where one party with the consent of the other, does some act inconsistent with the lease.

4. Merger

This occurs where a tenant acquires the estate of his landlord and the tenant's estate merges in the greater estate he has just acquired.

5. Forfeiture

A landlord cannot re-enter, i.e. recover possession from the tenant, for breach of a tenant's obligations unless the lease gives him the right, (usually by containing a proviso for re-entry on breach of covenant) or the lease is so drafted that observance of the covenants is a condition of the lease. The right of forfeiture may be waived either expressly or by implication. An implied waiver occurs if the landlord is aware of acts or omissions of a tenant which make the lease liable to forfeiture but still continues to recognise the existence of the lease, e.g. he accepts rent after knowing of a breach of covenant.

Where premises are let as a dwelling house, even if there is a forfeiture clause, a court order is still needed to evict a tenant.

a) Forfeiture for non-payment of rent

There must be a forfeiture clause or proviso for re-entry. The landlord must make a formal demand for rent unless there is half a year's rent unpaid and not sufficient distress on the premises i.e. not enough goods which can be sold to pay off the rent. Because it is a nuisance to comply with the legal requirements of making a formal demand for rent, most well-drafted leases will exempt a landlord from making a formal demand, e.g. 'provided always that if the rent is in arrears for 21 days, whether formally demanded or not, then it shall be lawful for the lessor to re-enter upon the premises and immediately thereupon the term shall absolutely determine.'

If the landlord brings an action for possession, the tenant has a discretionary right to relief provided he pays the arrears of rent and the costs of the proceedings. This remedy is available for up to six months after the judgment for possession. Where there are at least six months' arrears and the tenant pays all costs and arrears before the hearing, the action will be discontinued.

b) Forfeiture for breaches of other covenants

Again there must be a forfeiture clause. In addition the landlord must serve a notice on the tenant specifying the breach, requiring it to be remedied if possible and requiring compensation from the lessee for the breach, if appropriate.

If a repairing covenant has been broken in a lease of at least seven years of which three or more years remain unexpired, the landlord must, in addition, inform the tenant of his right to serve a counter-notice under the Leasehold Property Repairs Act, 1938. The landlord must then obtain leave of the County Court before proceeding further.

If a covenant against sub-letting or assigning or using the property for immoral purposes has been broken, then the covenant cannot be remedied. The landlord only has to serve a notice specifying the breach and the tenant has no claim to relief.

For breaches of most covenants other than sub-letting, assigning or using for immoral purposes, the tenant can apply for relief from forfeiture. Special rules apply depending on the type of property where there is provision for the landlord to re-enter on the bankruptcy of the tenant.

Underleases

If the headlease is forfeited, any underlease ceases, but whatever the ground on which a headlease was forfeited, an underlessee may seek relief against forfeiture. The court may order that the former underlessee hold the lease directly from the landlord for a term not exceeding the length of the original term.

E. RIGHTS AND OBLIGATIONS OF LANDLORD AND TENANT

Many leases will be formal documents in which the obligations of the landlord and the tenant are clearly stated. Sometimes reference will be made to usual covenants. What these are depends on the kind of property being let and the practice of conveyancers in the area. In the absence of express or usual covenants certain covenants are implied.

1. Implied obligations of the landlord

a) The landlord impliedly covenants that the tenant shall have quiet enjoyment of the property i.e. freedom from interference from the landlord or persons deriving title from him. The covenant does not mean freedom from noise.

PEREIRA v. VANDIYAR [1953] 1 WLR 672 C.A.

A landlord was *held* liable in damages under this covenant when he cut off gas and electricity supplies to the premises.

Under section 1 of the Protection from Eviction Act, 1977 it is also a criminal offence to evict unlawfully or harass a tenant.

b) The landlord must not derogate from his grant i.e. he must not render the property unfit for the purpose for which it was let.

c) Where it is a furnished letting of a house or flat, there is an implied warranty of fitness for habitation at the start of the tenancy.

d) Where a house or part of a house is let at a rent of not more than £80 per annum in London, or £52 elsewhere, there is an implied obligation of fitness for habitation at the start of the tenancy and throughout the term. For the landlord to be liable he must have been given notice of any defect.

e) By section 32 of the Housing Act, 1961 — in a lease of a dwelling house for a term of less than seven years, there is an implied covenant by the lessor, notwithstanding any agreement to the contrary:
   (i) to keep in repair the structure and exterior of the dwelling house including drains, gutters and external pipes.
   (ii) to keep in repair and proper working order the installations in the dwelling house for supply of water, gas, electricity, and for sanitation, including basins, sinks, baths; lavatories and for space heating and heating water.

2. Implied obligations of the tenant

a) to pay rent and tenant's rates and taxes.

b) to repair. The extent of the obligation to repair depends on the type of the tenancy although all tenants are liable if they wantonly alter the nature of the property (voluntary waste).

  (i) if it is a periodic tenancy the tenant must use the property in a tenant-like manner i.e. taking proper care of the property.

  (ii) if it is a fixed term tenancy the tenant is liable for permissive waste i.e. damage caused by neglecting the property e.g. letting the premises go to ruin.

F. EXPRESS COVENANTS

Express covenants can be drafted to cover all manner of situations. There will be covenants to pay rent and repair. The extent of the repairing obligations will depend on how the covenant is drafted. This covenant may oblige the lessee to re-build subsidiary parts of the premises where this is the only way of repairing but he cannot be compelled to re-build the premises completely. If the lessee covenants to repair 'fair wear and tear excepted' although he will not be liable for the fair wear and tear he will be liable for any damage which results e.g. if a skylight becomes defective the lessee will not be liable but he will be liable for any damage to the interior which results from rain leaking through the skylight. Section 18(1) of the Landlord and Tenant Act, 1927 provides that the amount of damages for the breach of a repairing covenant are not to exceed the amount by which the value of the reversion is diminished.

Another express covenant often found in leases is a covenant not to assign or underlet the premises. Such a covenant is construed restrictively. If the covenant is 'not to assign or underlet without the consent of the landlord' then section 19(1) of the Landlord and Tenant Act, 1927 implies that such consent will not be unreasonably withheld notwithstanding any agreement to the contrary. If however, the covenant against assignment and underletting is absolute, then the lessee cannot assign or underlet.

G. ENFORCEMENT OF COVENANTS IN LEASES

A covenant is a contractual agreement made by a covenantor in favour of a covenantee and contained in a deed. Besides being enforceable on a contractual basis, in some circumstances covenants are enforceable by and against third parties and are regarded as interests in land.

1. Privity of contract

Between the original landlord and original tenant there is privity of contract. All the covenants in the lease are enforceable by the landlord against the tenant and vice versa. The tenant remains liable throughout the term even after he has assigned his lease.

2. Privity of estate

Between the landlord for the time being and the tenant for the time being there is privity of estate.

When the tenant assigns the lease the assignee takes subject to the benefit and the burden of the covenants which 'touch and concern' the lease. There is no definition of what these covenants are but they affect the quality or value of the land, or the mode of using it, e.g. the assignee would be bound by covenants to pay rent, to repair, to insure against fire, to use as a dwelling house only, and not 'to assign or sublet without consent'. The assignee would be entitled to the benefit of covenants by the landlord to supply the demised premises with water, not to build on adjoining land, not to determine a periodic tenancy during its first three years and a covenant to renew the lease. A covenant to sell the reversion does not touch and concern the lease. It is outside the relationship of landlord and tenant.

An assignee is only liable for breaches of covenant while he has the lease and is not liable for breaches occuring before or after the assignment.

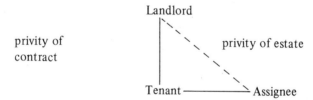

3. Indemnity

If the landlord sues the original tenant for breach of covenant committed by the assignee the tenant will want to claim indemnity. He can claim indemnity from the person to whom he assigned the property if, in the deed of assignment, there was an indemnity clause. If the assignment was for value, statute will imply such an indemnity clause. Where there have been several assignments of the lease e.g. T assigns to A who assigns to B who assigns to C and C is in breach, T can seek indemnity direct from C basing his claim in quasi-contract under the rule in *Moule* v. *Garrett* (1872) LR7 Ex 101.

4. Position of landlord

Where the reversion is assigned, it is the new landlord not the old who should enforce (and be bound by) the covenants, which touch and concern the lease, even for those breaches of covenant which took place before the assignment.

Example:

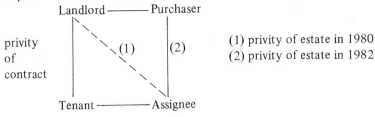

In 1976 the landlord granted a lease to the tenant. In 1980 the tenant assigned his lease to the assignee. In 1982 the landlord sold the reversion to the purchaser. After 1982 it is the purchaser who can sue for breaches of covenant, not the original landlord. Moreover, he can sue the tenant for breaches of covenant which the tenant committed before the reversion was sold to the purchaser even though there has never been at any stage privity of contract, or estate, between the purchaser and the original tenant. Should the assignee commit a breach of covenant, the purchaser has the option of either suing him or the original tenant. This modification of the contractual position where the landlord's reversion is sold is the result of judicial interpretation of section 141 of the Law of Property Act, 1925.

There is neither privity of contract nor estate between a head landlord and a sub-tenant.

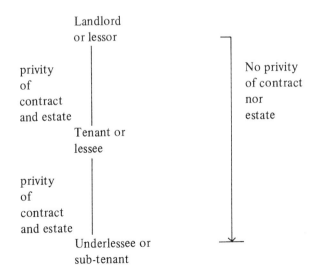

H. SECURITY OF TENURE AND RENT RESTRICTION

The contractual common law relationship between the parties has been modified by statute. Because of the uneven bargaining power between landlords and tenants, legislation has given tenants who fulfil certain requirements security of tenure at the end of the contractual term. Legislation has also restricted the amount of rent which can be claimed by a landlord.

1. Agricultural Holdings

These are governed by the Agricultural Holdings Act, 1948 as amended. An agricultural holding is land which is used for agriculture for the purposes of trade or business. A tenant of such a holding has security of tenure. Notice must be served by the landlord on the tenant not less than one year nor more than two years before the end of a fixed term tenancy. If not, it continues as a yearly tenancy. A full year's notice expiring on the anniversary of the commencement date is generally required to determine a yearly tenancy. In some circumstances, the tenant has a right to serve a counter-notice. Consent of the Agricultural Land Tribunal is then required before the landlord can obtain possession.

If certain conditions are fulfilled, a member of a deceased tenant's family can succeed to the holding.

Rent may be fixed by an arbitrator after a reference by either the landlord or the tenant. A tenant on quitting a holding, has a right to compensation for improvements. In some cases, a tenant is entitled to compensation for disturbance and a sum to enable him to re-organise his affairs.

2. Business tenancies

These are governed by the Landlord and Tenant Act, 1954 Part II. Business tenancies arise where premises are occupied by a tenant for purposes of his trade, business, profession or employment.

A landlord of business premises must give 6-12 months' notice to quit expiring not earlier than the contractual tenancy would have ended. Notice must be in the prescribed form. The tenant can give notice within two months that he is not willing to give up such possession. Then between two and four months after the landlord's notice, he can apply to the court for a new tenancy. A tenant holding for a fixed term can serve a notice on a landlord requiring a new tenancy to begin between 6 and 12 months later. The landlord has seven grounds on which to oppose a new tenancy. He must specify the ground in his statutory notice or in the notice served on the tenant in reply to the tenant's request for a new tenancy. The grounds on which a landlord can oppose a new tenancy are failure by the tenant to repair, pay rent or observe other covenants of the lease, or an offer by the landlord of alternative accommodation. If the landlord opposes on the three other grounds, namely that the premises let are part of a property and the property could be let better as a whole, or that the landlord wishes to demolish or reconstruct the premises, or he wants the premises for his own occupation (for this ground he must not have purchased the property within the last 5 years) then the tenant is entitled to compensation. The amount of compensation is equal to the rateable value of the premises, or twice the sum if the tenant, or his predecessors have occupied the premises for business purposes for the previous fourteen years. The tenant can also get compensation for improvements carried out by him if (1) the premises were let wholly or partly for business purposes, (2) the improvement added to the letting value of the premises and (3) notice of the proposed improvement was served on the landlord. The improvement must be made within the agreed time, and the claim for compensation must be made within three months of the act determining the tenancy.

If the landlord cannot establish the statutory grounds to oppose a new tenancy, the court can grant a tenancy for up to 14 years and can include such terms as it thinks fit.

3. Residential tenancies

These are governed by the Rent Act, 1977 as amended by the Housing Act, 1980.

Regulated tenancies

Where a dwelling house, or part of a house, is let as a separate dwelling, then a tenant will be protected under the Rent Acts, unless (1) the dwelling house is above certain specified rateable values, (2) no rent or a low rent is paid, (3) the dwelling house is let with other land, (4) rent includes board and attendance i.e. a service personal to the tenant, provided by the landlord, (5) the letting is to students by an authorised body e.g. a college, (6) it is a holiday letting, (7) the letting is of licensed premises, (8) it is an agricultural holding, (9) the landlord is a local authority housing association, housing co-operative or the Crown. (Protection is now given to public sector tenants under the Housing Act, 1980).

The main exception is where there is a resident landlord. This exception is to encourage people to let off extra rooms in their house without fear of the tenants obtaining full Rent Act protection.

Both a landlord and tenant under a protected tenancy have a statutory right to apply to the rent officer for a registration of a fair rent. The maximum sum then recoverable from the tenant is the registered rent. If the contractual rent is lower, until the contract is terminated, only that lower rent is payable.

At the end of the contractual term the tenant will be able to stay on in the premises as a statutory tenant. The nature of a statutory tenancy is that the tenant has no estate or interest in the land, but only a mere personal right of occupation. He cannot dispose of this interest by will or assignment and if he moves out of the property he will lose his interest. However, if a tenant dies while still a statutory tenant his or her spouse residing with the tenant at death or a member of his family who has resided with him for at least the previous six months, becomes a statutory tenant in his place. A second transmission is possible.

In order to obtain possession a landlord has to prove three things (1) that the contractual tenancy has been terminated, (2) that it is reasonable in all the circumstances for the landlord to obtain possession and (3) that he can establish a ground for possession under the Rent Act. There are some mandatory grounds for possession when the landlord does not need to prove (2) i.e. that it is reasonable for him to be granted possession. These grounds include homes of former owner-occupiers, retirement houses and the new Protected Shorthold Tenancies created by the Housing Act, 1980.

Restricted contracts

Where the landlord is resident on the premises the tenant has a restricted contract which only gives him limited protection.

The lessor, lessee or local authority can refer the contract to the rent tribunal for the determination of a reasonable rent. It is illegal to demand rent in excess of the registered rent.

The security given to a tenant depends on whether the contract was granted before or after the Housing Act. If before and a tenant has referred a contract to a Rent Tribunal which has power to approve, reduce or increase rent, no notice to quit subsequently served on him can take effect before six months from the decision of the tribunal. The tribunal may reduce the security if the tenant has been guilty of mis-conduct. If, however, a landlord serves a notice to quit first, the tenant can, before that notice expires, apply to the rent tribunal which can extend the period specified by the notice for up to six months.

These security provisions have no application where the letting is for a fixed term. No notice to quit is required to determine a fixed term so that the rent tribunal machinery for postponing the notice to quit has no application.

The only protection given to tenants of restricted contracts granted after 1980 and whose contracts have expired is to apply to the Court for a postponement of any possession order for up to 3 months. This very limited security is available to tenants of both fixed terms and periodic lettings. The tribunal jurisdiction is abolished for this purpose.

It should be noted that under the Protection from Eviction Act, 1977 a court order is always necessary to obtain possession where there is a residential occupier.

LEASEHOLD REFORM ACT, 1967

This act enables tenants who fulfil certain conditions to buy the freehold. The principle behind the legislation was that the tenant had in effect paid for the property at the start of the lease with a premium or capital sum. It has been criticised by many as amounting to expropriating the landlord without compensation.

In order to qualify the tenancy must be for over 21 years at a low rent within a specified rateable value. It must be a tenancy of a house, not a flat, and the tenant must have occupied the house as his only or main residence during the past 5 years or for periods totalling 5 during the past ten years.

The price the tenant will pay is the value of the property on the open market on the basis that it is subject to a fifty year lease.

As an alternative, the tenant can ask for a new lease for 50 years to take effect after the expiration of the tenant's existing lease. The rent will be the current letting value of the site only with a possible revision after 25 years.

7 Licences

OUTLINE

A. Types of Licence

1. Bare licence
2. Licence coupled with a grant
3. Contractual licence
4. Licences by estoppel

Can they be revoked?
Do they bind third parties?

B. Leases and Licences

1. Importance of distinction
2. Guidelines for making distinction

INTRODUCTION

A licence is a permission given by the occupier of land which allows the licensee to do something which would otherwise be a trespass. A licence may amount to the occupation of land or merely to a right to cross land. The law of licences is a developing branch of the law and shows equity at its most flexible.

A. TYPES OF LICENCE

1. A bare or gratuitous licence. This is a mere permission to the licensee to enter upon the licensor's land, e.g. to play cricket on a field. There is no element of consideration. The licence can be revoked at any time and will not bind a third party. The licensee cannot assign the benefit.

2. A licence coupled with a grant or interest. Such a licence arises where someone has been granted an interest in land or a chattel lying on the land and is given permission to enter the land in order that he may enjoy that interest. e.g. A man is entitled to timber and is given permission to go onto another's land to cut and cart the timber away. Equity may grant an injunction to prevent the licensor revoking the licence contrary to the terms of the grant. If the interest is legal or an equitable interest which is registered as an estate contract both the interest and the licence will bind an assignee of the licensor.

3. Contractual licence. This is a licence, usually express, supported by consideration. Sometimes the Court will imply a contract from the circumstances.

TANNER v. TANNER [1975] 1 WLR

The plaintiff bought a house for his mistress and their twins. The defendant gave up her Rent Act protected flat to move in with him. When the plaintiff later evicted her the Court awarded her compensation for breach of a contractual licence.

At common law contractual licences could be revoked at any time. The only remedy for premature revocation was an action for damages for breach of contract.

WOOD v. LEADBITTER (1845) 13 H & W 838

The plaintiff bought an admission ticket to a race-course. He was ordered to leave by the defendant who was the servant of the steward of the course. The plaintiff refused to go and was physically removed, no more force being used than was reasonably necessary. His action for assault and false imprisonment failed. He became a trespasser the moment his licence was revoked.

Since the Judicature Acts, 1873, which gave the Courts power to apply equitable rules in the common law courts, a breach of contract can be restrained by injunction.

The orthodox view is that contractual licences cannot bind third parties. However, where the justice of the case so requires the courts have strained to hold that third parties are bound.

ERRINGTON v. ERRRINGTON [1952] 1 KB 290

A father bought a house for £750, paying £250 cash and borrowing £500 from a Building Society secured by a mortgage. He let his son and daughter-in-law live in the property and told them that if they paid the mortgage instalments he would convey the legal estate to them. This they did, and nine years later, before all the repayments were completed, the father died. He left the house to his widow. The son left the wife. She remained in occupation and continued to pay the instalments. The widow brought an action for possession against the daughter-in-law. *Held*, the son and daughter-in-law were licensees entitled to occupy the house as long as they paid the instalments and so the licence was binding on the widow.

This case was severely criticised in a later case in the House of Lords. Another way of dealing with the problem was found by holding that in certain circumstances a contractual licence will give rise to a constructive trust.

BINIONS v. EVANS [1972] Ch 539

In 1965 the trustees of an estate made a written agreement with the widow of a deceased servant allowing her to remain in possession of her house without rent in consideration of her maintaining the property and continuing in personal occupation. Two years later the estate was sold to the plaintiff who accepted a special clause in the contract protecting Mrs. Evans' possession. In consequence the price was reduced. The plaintiff served a notice to quit 6 months later and Mrs. Evans opposed this notice. Lord Denning considered she had a contractual licence giving rise to a constructive trust which would bind a purchaser with notice.

It is more likely that a licence will be held to be a licence by estoppel if justice requires that it should be enforced against a third party.

4. Licences by estoppel. Various equitable devices have been used to uphold the right of a person using land from being disturbed in such use by the legal owner or his successors.

(1)   Mutual benefit and burden.
      If there is an arrangement whereby neighbours agree to grant each other reciprocal benefits over their land one party cannot claim the benefit while escaping from his burden.

E.R. IVES INVESTMENTS LTD. v. HIGH [1967] 2 QB 379

H. bought a bombed building site and started to build a house on it. W. bought an adjoining site and started to build a block of flats. W's flats encroached on H's land. H objected but then an agreement was reached. W's encroachment could remain and in return H could have a right of way over W's land to the flats. W sold the flats to X who knew of the agreement. H built a garage, access to which could only be reached across X's land. X raised no objection to the garage or the use of X's land to get to it. X's land was sold by auction to I. The particulars of sale referred to H's right of way and the conveyance to I was made subject to it. *Held* that I could not stop H using the right of way.

(2)   Expenditure on another's land.
      If an owner encourages someone to spend money on the owner's land with the expectation that he will be allowed to stay there then equity will not allow that expectation to be defeated.

INWARDS v. BAKER [1965] 2 QB 29

A father encouraged his son to build a bungalow on the father's land. The son did so on the understanding that he would be able to live there for the rest of his life. The father died leaving his land to the trustees. The trustees claimed the bungalow. *Held* that the son had an equitable right to remain in the bungalow for as long as he liked.

Even where there is found to be a licence protecting the licensee against third parties the extent of such protection is discretionary depending on how the Court considers justice can best be achieved.

PASCOE v. TURNER [1979] 1 WLR 431

The plaintiff went off with another woman but assured his former mistress, the defendant, that the house where they had both been living should be hers. On the strength of this assurance the defendant spent money on repairs and decorating. The plaintiff then sought to turn her out. The Court *held* that the only way to give the defendant adequate protection was to transfer the legal estate to her.

(3) Acquiescence.
If an owner of land acquiesces in another using rights over his land then he will not subsequently be allowed to prohibit such use where it would be inequitable to do so.

CRABB v. ARUN DISTRICT COUNCIL [1976] Ch 179

The plaintiff relying on an agreement by the defendant Council to give access to and a right of way over their land, sold off the northern part of his land. The defendants then changed their mind so that the plaintiff was left without any means of access to the road. *Held* that the defendants were estopped by their conduct from denying this right of way.

B. LEASES AND LICENCES

It is often difficult to decide whether an agreement amounts to a lease or a licence. The distinction is important because:

1. A lease gives a lessee protection under the Rent Acts. A licence will at best only give limited statutory protection to a licensee. Thus it will be an advantage to a landlord to establish he has only granted a licence.
2. A legal lease is a right in rem. It will bind a purchaser of the reversion. If it is an equitable lease it can be registered as an estate contract under the Land Charges Act, 1972 and thus bind a purchaser. In registered land a lease will bind a purchaser either as a minor or overriding interest. The general rule is that a licence will not bind a third party. As we have seen, however, licences arising from estoppel principles and possibly some contractual licences will bind third parties who buy

with notice. Such licences cannot, however, be registered under the Land Charges Act.

3. A tenant under a lease has an interest in land. The landlord commits a trespass if he re-enters premises without the authority of the tenant. If it is only a licence the licensor, by entering, may commit a breach of contract but not a trespass.

4. A lease is irrevocable though it may be voidable for breach of covenant if it contains a forfeiture clause. A licence according to the traditional view, could be revoked at any time. Today the Courts will not allow a contractual licence to be revoked in breach of the terms of the contract nor a licence arising by estoppel.

Guidelines for deciding whether a lease or licence:

1. A lease must give exclusive possession. A licence may or may not do so. If there is no intention to create the relationship of landlord and tenant there will be no lease even with exclusive possession. On the other hand, if a document is called a licence, it may be a lease, if its effect is to grant exclusive possession and to establish a landlord and tenant relationship. Labels are not conclusive.

2. If there is an element of charity or there is a family arrangement, the Courts are more likely to find that the agreement is a licence rather than a lease.

3. The terms of the agreement may indicate a lease, rather than a licence e.g. payment of rent, with proviso for re-entry on non-payment, covenant for quiet enjoyment.

8 Covenants Between Freeholders

OUTLINE

A. Common Law

1. Contractual liability between original parties.
2. Assignment of the benefit.
3. Burden cannot pass directly.

B. In Equity

1. Burden runs if
   (a) negative.
   (b) covenantee has land which will benefit.
   (c) section 79 Law of Property Act, 1925 not excluded.
   (d) registered.
2. Benefit will pass if
   (a) annexation or
   (b) assignment or
   (c) building scheme.

C. Discharge of Restrictive Covenants

1. Unity of seisin.
2. Application to Lands Tribunal under section 84 of the Law of Property Act, 1925.
3. Application to County Court under s 165 Housing Act, 1957.

INTRODUCTION

Use and control of land is governed by the Town and Country Planning Acts and buildings are subject to Building Regulations. But as well as this public control the use of land can be regulated by covenants. We have seen that covenants in leases are binding because of privity of estate or contract. It is often desirable that covenants should be enforceable between freeholders e.g. A vendor owns two plots of land. He wishes to sell one plot and impose on the purchaser an obligation to keep the fence in repair and to use the property for residential purposes only. He can do this through privity of contract but how can he be sure that the benefit and the burden of the covenants will pass to his successors in title and those of the purchaser respectively? It is essential when discussing such a problem to deal separately with the passing of the benefit and the passing of the burden.

The burden of a covenant can only pass in equity. It has been argued that where the burden has passed the equitable rules must also be applied for the passing of the benefit. However in one important case the burden passed in equity and the common law rules (which are less complex than the equitable rules) were applied for the passing of the benefit.

A. COMMON LAW

1. The *benefit* of a covenant, whether it is positive or negative, will run with the land if
   (i) it touches and concerns the land of the covenantee i.e. the person to whom the benefit of the covenant was given.
   (ii) the original covenantee has a legal estate in the land.
   (iii) the person seeking to enforce the covenant has a legal estate, either freehold or leasehold, and is a successor in title to the original covantee.

It is also possible that under section 56 of the Law of Property Act, 1925 a person who is not a party to a deed can enforce the benefit provided he is named or comes within a specific description and the benefit is conferred on him in that deed, e.g.

A covenants with B for the benefit of B and adjoining owners. Any existing and identifiable adjoining owners can enforce the covenant.

2. The *burden* of a covenant, whether positive or negative, cannot pass at law. However various devices have been used to attach the burden to a successor in title to the covenantor.

(i) A chain of covenants e.g. V sells to P who covenants to maintain a fence. P sells to Q. P is still liable to V by privity of contract. P will therefore want an indemnity from Q. If Q fails to maintain the fence V can sue P. P will then sue Q. This is unsatisfactory, for one of the parties in the chain may disappear or one might neglect to take an indemnity covenant. Moreover the remedy is only damages and not specific performance.

(ii) If a long lease (originally created for at least 300 years of which not less than 200 are unexpired) is converted to a freehold under section 153 of the Law of Property Act, 1925 the freehold is subject to the covenants of the lease. An enfranchisement under the Leasehold Reform Act, 1967 has a similar result.

(iii) A successor of the covenantor may be bound under the principle that he who takes the benefit must be subject to the burden.

HALSALL v. BRIZELL [1957] Ch 169

Purchasers of plots on a building estate executed deeds of covenant which gave them the benefit of using roads but imposed on them and their successors in title, the liability for their upkeep. The condition for taking the benefit was the payment of contributions towards the maintenance of the roads.

B. IN EQUITY

1. The leading case on the passing of the *burden* in equity is:

TULK v. MOXHAY (1848) 2 Ch 774

The plaintiff sold a vacant site in Leicester Square to E. E covenanted on behalf of himself, his heirs and his assigns that he would keep and maintain that land 'in an open state, uncovered with any buildings, in neat and ornamental order'. Moxhay bought the land with notice of the covenant and began to build on the site. The plaintiff was granted an injunction restraining him from building because, as Moxhay had bought with notice, it would be unconscionable if he were not bound by the covenant.

2. The burden of a covenant will only pass today if —

(i) The covenant is negative in substance. It can be negative even if expressed positively. The test is 'does the covenant require expenditure of money?' If it does then it is positive.

(ii) The covenantee must have other land i.e. a dominant tenement, for the protection of which the covenant has been taken. Such land must be capable of being benefitted by the covenant. It has been held that a landlord has a sufficient interest to be able to enforce a restrictive covenant against a sub-tenant.

(iii) The burden of the covenant must have been intended to run with the covenantor's land. This will be implied by section 79 of the Law of Property Act, 1925 unless there is a contrary intention.

(iv) Since 1925 a restrictive covenant must be registered against the estate owner of the burdened land, or where the land is registered a note of such restrictive covenant must be entered in the charges register of the title of the burdened land. If not so registered or noted a successor in title of the covenantor will take free of the interest whether he knows of it or not.

3. The *benefit* of the covenant will pass in equity if there is

(i) Annexation.

If there is a clause in the deed creating the covenant which shows that the covenant is for the benefit of a particular piece of land, or is in favour of the vendor and his successors in title in their capacity as estate owners of the retained land then such a covenant will automatically run with the benefitted land on subsequent sales. If the area is greater than can reasonably be benefitted then the covenant cannot be effectively annexed nor will the covenant pass with a sale of part of the land where the benefit has been annexed to the whole of the land. However where the benefit is annexed to each and every part these problems do not arise. Moreover there is a general tendency today for the courts to interpret liberally the requirements of annexation. In the latest case on annexation *Federated Homes Ltd* v. *Mill Lodge Properties Ltd* [1980] 1 WLR 594 it was decided that section 78 Law of Property Act, 1925 had the effect of automatically annexing a covenant to each and every part of the covenantee's land provided the property to be benefitted was sufficiently identified.

(ii) Assignment.

The benefit of a covenant may be expressly assigned at the time of the sale of the covantee's land. It seems that on subsequent sales the benefit of the covenant will have to be expressly assigned. If the much-criticised case of *Federated Homes* is followed then there will be no need to rely on an express assignment of the benefit of the covenant.

(iii) Building schemes or schemes of development.

Often new housing estates will be built where, in order to keep up the tone of the neighbourhood, it is important that certain covenants be observed by purchasers of the individual plots, and their successors in title, and that such covenants should be enforceable by the plotholders amongst themselves.

In *Elliston* v. *Reacher [1908] 2 Ch 374* it was laid down that where (a) there was a common vendor (b) who laid out his property in lots (c) subject to restrictions which were to benefit all the plots sold and (d) the purchasers bought such land on the footing that the restrictions were for the benefit of all the plots, such restrictions would be mutually enforceable.

Since then the courts have held that it is not essential for all the requirements of *Elliston* v. *Reacher* to be fulfilled. All that is necessary is that there should be a common intention to create a local law for the area which will bind all purchasers. This local law will cover sub-purchasers.

C. DISCHARGE OF RESTRICTIVE COVENANTS

If the land subject to the burden and the land which is entitled to the benefit come into the same hands then the restrictive covenant will be extinguished. Where there is a building scheme however such unity of ownership only suspends the restrictive covenant. On a subsequent dividing of the land the covenant will revive.

In other cases it is possible to apply to the Lands Tribunal for the discharge of the covenant. The applicant must prove that the restrictive covenant is obsolete or obstructive to the user of the land or that the person entitled to the benefit of the covenant has agreed to, or will not be injured by its discharge.

Under s 165 of the Housing Act, 1957 an application can be made to the County Court to vary a restrictive covenant so that a house may be converted into two or more dwellings provided the applicant has planning permission for such conversion or can prove, that owing to changes in the neighbourhood, the house cannot be readily let as a whole.

9 Easements

OUTLINE

A. Essentials

1. Dominant and Servient Tenement.
2. Must be separately owned/occupied
3. Must accommodate the dominant tenement
4. Must be capable of forming the subject matter of a grant.

Compare with
  (i) public rights
 (ii) natural rights
(iii) restrictive covenants
(iv) licences
 (v) profits
(vi) principle of non-derogation of grant

B. Acquisition of Easements

1. Statute
2. Reservation
   (i) express
  (ii) implied
3. Grant
   (i) express
  (ii) implied
      (a) necessity
      (b) intention
      (c) Wheeldon v. Burrows (1879) 12 ChD 31
      (d) Section 62 Law of Property Act, 1925
 (iii) presumed
      (a) prescription at common law
      (b) lost modern grant
      (c) Prescription Act, 1832
          20 year user
          40 year user.

C. Special Rules for Acquisition of Light

D. Extent of Easements of Way

1. express
2. implied grant or reservation
3. prescription

E. Extinguishment of Easements

1. Express release
2. Implied release
3. Unity of ownership

INTRODUCTION

An easement is a private right enjoyed by successive owners and occupiers of land over neighbouring land, e.g. a right of way. It will be a legal easement if granted by deed for an estate equivalent to a fee simple absolute or a term of years. In any other case it will be equitable and in the case of unregistered land will need to be registered if it is to bind a purchaser of the servient tenement. It should be registered as a Class D(iii) land charge under the Land Charges Act, 1972.

A. ESSENTIALS

There are four essentials of an easement:

1. There must be a dominant tenement and a servient tenement. An easement cannot exist in gross for it must be concerned with the ownership of the land. The burden must be attached to one plot of land, i.e. the servient tenement, for the benefit of another, i.e. the dominant tenement.

2. The easement must accommodate the dominant tenement, i.e. it must improve the amenities of the tenement.

HILL v. TUPPER (1863) 2 HLC 121

The owner of a canal leased the bank of the canal to Hill and granted him the sole and exclusive right of putting boats on the canal. Tupper, without any authority, put rival boats on the canal. If Hill had an easement he could sue anyone who interfered with his right which would be a property right enforceable against all the world. *Held*: it was not an easement. As it was not appurtenant to land the right could only exist as a licence.

3. The dominant and servient tenements must be separately occupied. No one can have an easement over his own land. Quasi-easements are rights regularly exercised by a man over his own land, which, if the part in question were owned and occupied by another would be easement. They may subsequently become easements if the land is sold in separate parts.

4. The right must lie in grant, i.e. there must be a capable grantor and grantee and the right must be capable of forming the subject matter of a grant. It must not be too vague. The list of possible easements is not closed but there are limits.

PHIPPS v. PEARS [1965] 1 QB 76

The defendant demolished his house which ajoined that of the plaintiff. This left the plaintiff's house exposed to the weather. The plaintiff sought damages on the ground that he had an easement to be protected from the weather. He did not succeed in his claim to an easement.

The Courts are reluctant to uphold negative easements which restrict the servient owner's use of his land, or easements which involve the servient owner in expenditure of money. An exception is an easement requiring a neighbour to fence his land. This is sometimes referred to as a spurious easement. An easement must not amount to exclusive use of the property.

Easements distinguished from

(i) Public rights

A public right is exercisable by anyone whether he owns land or not. An easement has to be appurtenant to land. There is a public right to fish and navigate between high and low water marks when covered in water but no right to bathe, beachcomb or to walk.

There is a public right of way on highways. Highways can include unmetalled tracks. They can be created by statute or by 'dedication and acceptance'. At common law an informal dedication might arise through long user. If there is twenty years user there is a rebuttable presumption of dedication. Roads and paths are often blocked off one day a year to prevent such a presumption from arising.

There is no right to roam at common law but there are various statutes like The National Parks and Access to the Countryside Act, 1949 which give this right.

(ii) Natural rights

There is a natural right to the support of land. Natural rights exist automatically and are protected by the law of tort. There is no natural right to support for buildings, but if the withdrawing of such support would cause damage to the land, then damage to the building can be claimed as well. Support for buildings can be claimed as an easement.

There is no natural right to light. There is a natural right to water where it flows in a defined channel but no natural right to underground water which is not in a defined channel.

(iii) Restrictive covenants

Both easements and restrictive covenants enable a landowner to restrict the use of a neighbour's land. Both rights require a dominant and servient tenement. Easements however can be legal and can be obtained by long user. Restrictive covenants can only exist as equitable interests. They must be negative though they can be wider in scope than easements.

(iv) Licences

Licences are much more flexible than easements. They can permit all sorts of activities on land. A licence does not need a dominant tenement. Originally licences did not create an interest in land nor could they affect third parties.

(v) Profits

A profit is the right to take parts of the soil or produce from another's land, e.g. gravel, grass or crops. A profit can exist 'in gross', i.e. there does not have to be a dominant tenement.

(vi) The principle of non-derogation of grant

A person who sells or lets land, knowing that a purchaser wants it for a particular purpose, may not do anything which hinders that purpose. He cannot take away with one hand what he has given with the other. This principle will bind the grantor and all those who claim under him.

B. ACQUISITION OF EASEMENTS

1. By statute

Private Acts or Public Acts of Parliament can confer easements, e.g. Electricity Boards are granted easements to lay cables, or local authorities to put in sewers.

2. By reservation

When a vendor conveys property he can reserve across the property sold an easement for himself.

| Vendor
Plot I | Purchaser |
| | Plot II |

Example: A vendor owns Plots I and II. He sells Plot II to a purchaser and reserves to himself a right of way across Plot II.

In exceptional cases there will be an implied reservation in favour of the vendor. There are very few cases because if a vendor wishes to reserve easements he should do so expressly. Easements of necessity, e.g. where the vendor's retained land is landlocked and possibly intended easements, e.g. rights of support, may be implied.

3. By grant

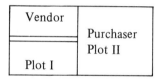

Example: A vendor may own Plots I and II and on the sale of Plot II to the purchaser may expressly grant him a right of way over Plot I which is retained by the vendor.

Easements of necessity and intention will be implied in favour of the purchaser more readily than are reserved in favour of a vendor.

WONG v. BEAUMONT PROPERTY TRUST LTD. [1965] 1 QB 173

A landlord leased a basement property to a tenant for use as a restaurant. The plaintiff took an assignment of the property from the tenant. He covenanted to comply with the Public Health Regulations. Later the plaintiff discovered that such compliance would involve installing a ventilation system in the upstairs premises which belonged to the defendant, who had bought the landlord's interest. *Held*: that the plaintiff had an easement of necessity to do this otherwise he would not be able to comply with the regulations.

Under the rules in *Wheeldon* v. *Burrows* where a vendor sells part of his land, the purchaser will have rights over the vendor's retained land if (a) such rights were previously used by the vendor for the benefit of the land conveyed, and either (b) they were reasonably necessary for the land conveyed, or (c) were continuous and apparent.

Section 62 of the Law of Property Act, 1925 provides that a conveyance of land will operate to convey all rights, privileges and easements enjoyed with the land at the time of the conveyance. Thus the Section has a similar effect to *Wheeldon* v. *Burrows* but is restricted to passing rights by conveyance while the Rule in *Wheeldon* v. *Burrows* can also apply to contracts and wills. Another limitation on section 62 is that there has to be some diversity of ownership or occupation of the quasi-dominant and servient tenement before the conveyance.

Examples: S. owns plots I and II. S intends to lease Plot I to D. D goes into possession and is given permission to cross Plot II. S executes a lease (which counts as a conveyance). The permission to cross Plot II is converted into an easement which will last as long as the lease.

S leases Plot I to D. S gives D permission to cross Plot II. S sells fee simple of Plot I to D. D will then have an easement.

The right does not have to be reasonable and necessary nor continuous and apparent for the purposes of Section 62 (c.f. *Wheeldon* v. *Burrows*).

Presumed grant

The Courts are anxious to uphold long established uses of land. Thus they will presume that a grant of a legal easement was once made.

For all forms of prescription the user must have been continuous and must have been used by a fee simple owner against a fee simple owner. So if the land is leased at the beginning of the user there can be no question of prescription. If the property is leased subsequently, it does not affect the user.

The user must be as of right. The doctrine rests on the presumption that there was a grant, so if there is any evidence to the contrary the presumption will be defeated. It is said that the user must be *nec vi* (without physical force), *nec clam* (without secrecy), *nec precario*, (without permission.) Any form of permission will defeat a claim to prescription at Common Law though there may be a sufficient user after the permission has expired.

For prescription at Common Law there must have been user since 1189. User for 20 years raises a rebuttable presumption. Evidence may show that user could not have existed since that date or that there has not been user during that time, e.g. it will be difficult to establish for a building a common law right to light as most buildings would not have existed in 1189.

Where user cannot be shown since 1189 sometimes reliance has been placed on a 'Lost Modern Grant'. This is a fiction that there was a grant but that this has been lost. For this doctrine to be relied on there must be 20 years user as of right and a possible grantor.

Some of the difficulties of Common Law prescription were dealt with by the Prescription Act, 1832. This Act provides two different times for prescription, a twenty year period and a forty year period. User for twenty years may establish a right but it can be defeated by a number of grounds. User for forty years gives an absolute and indefeasible right unless enjoyed by written consent.

User for twenty years cannot be defeated by proof that the user began after 1189, but it can be defeated if it does not comply with the other Common Law requirements. Thus user must be against a fee simple owner, by and on behalf of a fee simple owner and it must be user as of right. Oral or written consent given at the beginning or during the course of the user will defeat the claim. Any time during which the owner of the servient land is a minor, lunatic or tenant for life is excluded from the computation of the twenty-year period.

Written but not oral consent given at the beginning of the user will defeat a claim to the 40 year period as will any form of consent given during the user. Any time during which the servient land was leased for a term exceeding 3 years is deducted from the 40 year period provided the claim to the easement is resisted by the servient owner within three years of the ending of the lease.

The 20 or 40 year enjoyment of a right under the Prescription Act must have immediately preceded a Court action either claiming or denying the right.

Example: A right of way is enjoyed for 50 years by X. Then the right of way is barred. X does not object for 2 years. His claim to an easement will then be defeated. However, if he acquiesces in the interruption for less than a year, he can claim the easement.

C. SPECIAL RULES FOR THE ACQUISITION OF LIGHT BY PRESCRIPTION

There is no natural right to light but a right can be acquired by prescription. Rules for prescription are much easier in relation to light. The period of user is 20 years and this period gives an indefeasible right i.e. it is equivalent to 40 years user for other forms of easement. The rules are more lax. The user does not have to be by a fee simple owner against a fee simple owner nor does the user have to be as of right. Unity of possession which would extinguish a claim to any other form of easement, merely suspends the running of time in a claim to an easement of light. No deductions are made for periods when the servient owner is a lessee, lunatic, tenant for life or a minor.

Under the Rights of Light Act, 1959 a servient owner can register a notice in the local Land Charges Register, preventing anyone claiming a right of light.

The amount of light a person can claim under an easement is what is needed for the ordinary purposes of the building for which the right is being claimed.

ALLEN v. GREENWOOD [1979] 1 ALL ER 819

A man put a greenhouse at the end of his garden. The next-door neighbour was planning an extension to his house which would prevent light from reaching the greenhouse. There would still be enough light to read a newspaper but not enough for growing tomatoes. *Held*: the ordinary use of a greenhouse requires more light than a sitting room. Alternatively there was a right by prescription to claim an extra-ordinary amount of light, provided it was enjoyed for the full period of 20 years to the knowledge of the servient owners.

D. EXTENT OF EASEMENTS

The extent of the easement depends on how it is acquired. An express grant or reservation depends on the construction of the document. An implied grant depends on the user when the right arose. If the easement arises by prescription then that kind of user must have existed for the requisite period. Intensification does not alter the kind of user. e.g. if there has been 20 years user of a right of way for caravans it does not matter if the number of caravans is increased during the period from 6 to 30.

E. EXTINGUISHMENT OF EASEMENTS

An express release by deed or in writing supported by consideration will extinguish an easement. In some cases an oral release may be binding on general equitable grounds, e.g. Where D has orally agreed to release an easement of light and S has spent money on a building which has obstructed D's light.

A release may be implied from surrounding circumstances. Non user for 20 years might raise a presumption, but this could be rebutted if the dominant owner could show he had no intention to give up his right. Destroying a building might show evidence of intention to abandon a right to light.

10 Mortgages

OUTLINE

A. Creation of Mortgages

1. Legal
   (a) by demise
   (b) by legal charge

2. Equitable
   (a) Legal estate by informal means or where no intention to create legal mortgage
   (b) Mortgage of an equitable interest must be equitable.

B. Mortgagor's Right of Redemption

1. No irredeemability
2. No option to purchase
3. No excessive postponement
4. No collateral advantages
5. No oppressive or unconscionable terms
6. No restraint of trade
7. No extortionate bargains under Consumer Credit Act.

C. Mortgagee's Remedies

1. Sue on personal covenant
2. Foreclosure
3. Sale
4. Possession
5. Appointment of a receiver.

D. Protection of Mortgagee Against Subsequent Purchasers or Mortgagees

1. Title deeds
2. Registration

E. Discharge of Mortgage

Receipt.

INTRODUCTION

A mortgage is a loan secured on property so that if the mortgagor, that is the borrower, defaults, then the lender, who is called the mortgagee, will have a charge on the property itself which he can sell and the debt will then be paid out of the proceeds of sale. A purchaser when buying a home will often obtain a mortgage from a building society.

The loan is normally repayable over a long term of years. If it is an instalment mortgage periodic payments of capital and interests will be paid to the mortgagee. An alternative form of mortgage is where the capital sum is not repayable until the end of the mortgage term. The mortgagor will in the meantime pay interest on the capital debt.

A. CREATION OF A MORTGAGE

It has been said that no one by the light of nature ever understood an English mortgage. A legal mortgage can be created by demise. The mortgagor grants a lease usually of 3000 years to the mortgagee with a condition that when the debt is repaid the term will come to an end. Alternatively a legal charge can be executed which gives the mortgagee the same powers and remedies as if he had a mortgage by demise.

Legal charges are better than mortgages by demise because they are cheaper and simpler. Leaseholds and freeholds can be charged together. Where there is a mortgage, as distinct from a charge, of leasehold property the mortgage operates as a sub-demise. If there is a provision in a lease against sub-letting it seems therefore that a mortgage might amount to a breach of this covenant whilst a charge would not, as no actual estate is confered on the chargee.

Equitable mortgages of a legal estate arise where mortgages are created informally. A written memorandum will be needed to satisfy s 40 of the Law of Property Act, 1925 unless the deeds have been deposited with the mortgagee. A deposit of title deeds amounts to part performance and is often used where a customer wants an overdraft from the bank.

Any mortgage of an equitable interest must be equitable e.g. a life interest under a settlement or an equitable interest held under a trust for sale.

B. MORTGAGOR'S RIGHT OF REDEMPTION

The mortgage deed provides when the money is to be repaid. This is usually six months after the date of the deed and is totally fictitous as the mortgagor is not expected to be able to repay the loan by this date. It is only put so early because it is from that date that most of the mortgagees remedies are available. Equity has intervened to ensure that the mortgagor can redeem his property after the contractual redemption date free of any oppressive terms of the mortgage. It is said that there must be 'no clogs on the equity.' Thus:

(1) there must be no irredeemability. It would be inconsistent with the nature of a mortgage that it should be irredeemable, or that the right to redeem should be confined to certain persons or to a limited period, or to part only of the property. Any express stipulation inconsistent with the right of redemption will be ineffective.

(2) a mortgage cannot be converted into a sale of the mortgaged property by the mortgagee exercising an option to purchase given in the mortgage deed. However an option given later is valid and enforceable for the borrower has already obtained the money and is not subject to the same pressures to agree to the mortgagee's demands.

(3) although a provision postponing the date of redemption may be valid an excessive postponement may in itself be oppressive and therefore a clog on the equity of redemption.

FAIRCLOUGH v. SWAN BREWERY CO. LTD. [1912] AC 565

A 20 year lease was mortgaged and there was a condition in the mortgage preventing the redemption until six weeks before the end of the term. *Held*: the condition made the right to redeem illusory because the property could not be redeemed until the lease was nearly over and the redemption was not worth having. The mortgagor was allowed to redeem after only three years.

c.f. KNIGHTSBRIDGE ESTATES TRUST LTD. v. BYRNE [1939] Ch 441.

The plaintiffs mortgaged a large number of properties to the defendant insurance company. The repayments were half-yearly instalments repayable over 40 years. The mortgagees agreed not to call in the money in advance of the due dates. Six years later the plaintiffs asked for a declaration that they should be able to redeem the mortgage. *Held*: they could not. This was a fair bargain between business men.

(4) the redemption must be free of the conditions of the mortgage. Redemption must be complete redemption so that the mortgagor is restored

to his original position. A mortgagee's collateral advantages are valid until redemption but not afterwards.

NOAKES AND CO. LTD. v. RICE [1902] AC 24

On the mortgage of a public house the mortgagor covenanted to sell only the mortgagee's beer. During the mortgage the mortgagor was bound by the covenant but not after redemption. He had mortgaged a free house and was entitled to have it back as a free not a tied house.

Similarly in

BRADLEY v. CARRITT [1903] AC 253

The mortgagor mortgaged to a tea broker the shares which gave him a controlling interest in a tea company. The mortgagor guaranteed that the mortgagee should always remain broker to the tea company. The mortgagor, having paid off the mortgage, was *held* to be free from this unlimited guarantee.

However, if the collateral advantage is part of a complex business deal between traders the courts are reluctant to upset the bargain made by the parties.

KREGLINGER v. NEW PATAGONIA MEAT AND COLD STORAGE CO. LTD. [1914] AC 25

A mortgage by a meat company contained a condition that for five years the company should not sell sheep skins to any other person without first offering them to the woolbrokers. The mortgage was re-paid after two years and the defendants claimed they should no longer be bound by this condition. *Held* by the House of Lords that they continued to be bound.

(5) oppressive and unconscionable terms will be invalidated.

CITYLAND AND PROPERTY (HOLDINGS) LTD. v. DABRATH [1979] Ch 84

Instead of interest the defendant was required to pay off the loan by monthly instalments which included an additional sum described by the plaintiff as a premium. The entire capital sum lent was repayable on default and it was calculated that the premium amounted to the equivalent of interest at 57%. The Court *held* that the plaintiffs should be entitled to their capital and interest at 7%. The provision for payment of the premium was unconscionable.

Contrast however *Multiservice Bookbinding Co.* v. *Marsden* [1974] Ch 84 where the Court upheld an interest rate which was 2% above the Minimum Lending Rate and in addition index-linked to the Swiss franc. Although this resulted in an unreasonable gain to the mortgagees it was held not to be unconscionable being a business deal between equal partners.

(6) a term must not be in restraint of trade.

ESSO PETROLEUM v. HARPER'S GARAGE (STOURPORT) LTD. [1968] AC 269

A borrower mortgaged a garage, to secure a loan repayable over 21 years and not before. He covenanted to buy only Esso Fuel. Three years later he began to get his supplies from elsewhere and wanted to repay the loan. *Held* that the restraint of trade doctrine applied in mortgage deeds and that as it was unreasonable it was void.

(7) a term must not amount to an extortionate credit bargain under ss 137 to 139 The Consumer Credit Act, 1974. If so the Court may re-open the bargain to do justice between the parties. These sections apply to any mortgage but the other provisions of the Consumer Credit Act regulating mortgages are directed towards second mortgages and only apply to loans of under £5,000 not granted by building societies, local authorities, insurance companies or friendly societies.

These rules, both common law and statutory, protect the mortgagor against the mortgagee. In return the mortgagor who wishes to redeem must give the mortgagee notice, usually six months, or interest in lieu, to enable the mortgagee to find another investment for his capital.

C. MORTGAGEE'S REMEDIES

If the mortgagor defaults on the repayment of capital several remedies are available to the mortgagee. Once the money is contractually due he can sue on the personal covenant to repay the loan given by the mortgagor in the mortgage deed. This remedy will be of limited value if the mortgagor has no money with which to repay the loan. The mortgagee can also seek a foreclosure order from the court. Foreclosure has the effect of extinguishing the equity of redemption i.e. the rights which the mortgagor retains in the mortgaged property. These rights include his equitable right to redeem the property after the contractual redemption date. The legal estate is vested in the mortgagee subject to any earlier mortgages but free of the interests of any subsequent ones. The court first grants an order nisi directing that accounts be taken and that the mortgagor shall pay off the sums due. If he defaults then an order absolute is made. The foreclosure can be re-opened if the mortgagor can show that the property had some special personal value to him or that he was prevented from paying the money because of some accident.

The Court has power to order a sale instead of foreclosure, on the application of any interested party. This is likely if there are subsequent mortgagees or if the value of the property exceeds the amount of the debt.

Because of the unfairness of the effect of foreclosure it is more usual for the mortgagee to apply for a sale of the property. The power of sale arises where the mortgage is by deed and the money is due i.e. the original redemption date has passed, provided the power of sale is not excluded in the mortgage deed. However this power can only be exercised if notice has been served on the mortgagor requiring payment and default has continued for three months, or interest under the mortgage is in arrear for two months, or there has been a breach of another covenant in the mortgage deed. A purchaser is only concerned to see that the power has *arisen*. He is not concerned to see if it is *exerciseable*. If the power is not exerciseable the mortgagee will be liable in damages to the mortgagor but the purchaser will obtain a good title.

A mortgagee is not a trustee of the power of sale, although he must make a genuine sale. He owes a duty of care to obtain a proper price.

CUCKMERE BRICK CO. LTD. v. MUTUAL FINANCE LTD, [1971] CL 945.

The mortgagee advertised the property without mentioning that the land had valuable planning permission. *Held* that the mortgagee was accountable to the mortgagor, for the difference between a proper price and the price obtained.

The Building Society's Act, 1962 provides that a building society must obtain the *best* price reasonably obtainable.

A mortgagee is a trustee of any surplus proceeds of sale. He should search under the Land Charges Act, 1972 for subsequent mortgages before handing any surplus proceeds to the mortgagor.

If a mortgagee is going to sell the property charged he will want to obtain possession so that he can sell it free of the occupancy of the mortgagor. He might also want to take possession to preserve the property or to obtain any income produced by the property. Theoretically a mortgagee can take possession of the mortgaged property at any time after the execution of the mortgage. Usually he will not wish to do this as he will be liable for wilful default.

WHITE v. CITY OF LONDON BREWERY CO. (1889) 42 Ch D 237

The mortgagor mortgaged a public house as a free house. The mortgagee, a brewer, took possession and let the house as a 'tied' house. He was *held* liable for the additional rent he would have obtained if he had let the property as a 'free' house.

Normally a court order is necessary before a mortgagee can take possession. Under the Administration of Justice Acts, 1970 and 1973 the court may delay the exercise of the mortgagee's right to possession where the mortgaged property is a dwelling house if this might help the mortgagor to make good his default.

Instead of taking possession, where a mortgagee is anxious to receive income from the property he may appoint a receiver. As the receiver is deemed to be the agent of the mortgagor this imposes less responsibility on the mortgagee than taking possession.

The remedies available to an equitable mortgagee depend on whether the mortgage was created by deed. If it has been so created then the mortgagee can sell the property, though he will need the appropriate conveyancing device to be able to sell the legal estate, and appoint a receiver. It is controversial whether or not without express authority he can take possession of the property. Even without a deed the mortgagee can apply to the court for an order of foreclosure or for sale or for the appointment of a receiver.

D. PROTECTION OF MORTGAGES AGAINST SUBSEQUENT PURCHASERS OR MORTGAGEES

A first mortgagee of property is entitled to the title deeds whether the mortgage is legal or equitable. Subsequent mortgagees who do not obtain the title deeds must in unregistered land register a *puisne* mortgage i.e. a legal mortgage not protected by deposit of title deeds, or a general equitable charge where the mortgage is equitable under the Land Charges Act. In registered land such mortgages will be protected by an entry on the register.

Thus a subsequent purchaser or mortgagee will have notice of the first mortgage either because of the absence of title deeds or because of a registered Land Charge under The Land Charges Act, 1972 or entry in the register under The Land Registration Act, 1925.

E. DISCHARGE OF MORTGAGE

A receipt on a mortgage will discharge the mortgage if it states the name of the payer and names the mortgagee. If the payer is not the mortgagor, or his trustee, the effect is to transfer the benefit of the mortgage to him. Thus the mortgagor's land will be subject to a secured loan in favour of the payer, who becomes the mortgagee.

11 Registration

OUTLINE

A. Registration of Incumbrances in Unregistered Land

1. Purposes
   (a) enables a purchaser to discover incumbrances
   (b) protects an owner of such incumbrances
2. Registers: most important of charges
   (a) legal mortgages not protected by title deed
   (b) equitable mortgages not protected by title deeds
   (c) estate contracts
   (d) restrictive covenants entered into after 1925
   (e) equitable easements
   (f) a spouse's right of occupation under the Matrimonial Homes Act, 1967
3. Effect of registration and non-registration
4. Official certificate of search

B. Registration of Title

1. Purposes
   (a) to prevent separate investigation of title on every transfer of land
   (b) to give a state guaranteed title
2. Classes of interest
   (a) registered interests
   (b) overriding interests
   (c) minor interest
      (1) notices
      (2) cautions
      (3) inhibitions
      (4) restrictions
3. Parts of the register
   (a) property
   (b) proprietorship
   (c) charges

4. Types of title
   (a) freeholds
        (i) absolute
        (ii) possessory
        (iii) qualified
   (b) leasehold
   (c) upgrading title
5. Searches
6. Rectification
7. Indemnity

INTRODUCTION

It is important to realise that there are two distinct systems of registration. There is registration of incumbrances in the land charges register which applies where the title to land is unregistered. And there is registration of title under the Land Registration Act, 1925.

A. REGISTRATION OF INCUMBRANCES IN UNREGISTERED LAND

1. Purposes

In unregistered land certain incumbrances are registrable under the Land Charges Act, 1972 against the names of estate owners whose land is subject to the burden. The purpose of such registration is that (a) it enables a purchaser when investigating title to discover easily whether certain incumbrances exist, (b) it protects the owner of such incumbrances against defeat by a purchaser of the legal estate.

In other words it helps to hold the balance between the interest of a purchaser and the owner of a third party right. The doctrine of notice is replaced by registration for those rights specified in the Land Charges Act, 1972.

2. Registers

Registers are kept of land charges, pending actions, writs and orders affecting land, annuities and deeds of arrangement affecting land. The most important register is the land charges register, and the most important charges are comprised in class C, D and F of that register.

Class C includes,
a. a *puisne* mortgage which is a legal mortgage not protected by deposit of title deeds. This charge is unusual in that it is not an equitable interest but a legal interest which has to be registered in order to bind third parties.
b. a general equitable interest which,
   i) is an equitable charge not secured by the deposit of title deeds of

the legal estate affected,

   ii) does not arise or affect an interest arising under a trust for sale or a settlement and

   iii) is not included in any other class of registrable interest.

The most usual charge would be an equitable mortgage of a legal estate where the title deeds are not deposited with the mortgagee.

c. an estate contract which is a contract by an estate owner to convey a legal estate. It includes contracts for the sale of a fee simple, contracts for leases and options to renew a lease and options to purchase the freehold reversion.

Class D includes,

a. restrictive covenants entered into after 1925 and not made between lessor and lessee. Thus a restrictive covenant in a lease is not registrable under the Land Charges Act.

b. an equitable easement arising after 1925. The difficulty about this class of easement is that it would include informal arrangements between neighbours who would not be aware of the need to register their interests.

A Class F land charge which is the right of a spouse in whom the legal estate is not vested i.e., the spouse's name does not appear on the title deeds, to register his or her right of occupation. This right arises on marriage and is not conditional on desertion. It does not apply to co-habitees.

This Class F charge, created by the Matrimonial Homes Act, 1967 is unsatisfactory in many ways. It is unrealistic to expect non-owning spouses to register as usually they will not know of their right and even if they do it could provoke hostility between the partners in the marriage should such a charge be registered. To register a charge a spouse would need to know whether or not the property was registered.

3. Effect of registration and non-registration

Registration of a land charge is notice of that charge to all persons for all purposes. A *puisne* mortgage, a general equitable charge and a spouse's statutory right of occupation if not registered will be void against a purchaser for value of *any* interest in the land. Estate contracts, restrictive covenants and equitable easements are only void against a purchaser for *money* or *money's worth of a legal estate*.

4. Searches

When buying unregistered land the vendor will supply a title to the property tracing the devolution of the legal estate back to a conveyance at least 15 years old. The purchaser should search against the name of the vendor, and all other estate owners who held the land during the period covered by the abstracted title to see if there are any incumbrances registered against those names. The result of the search is conclusive in favour of the purchaser and if he completes his purchase within 15 days of the date of the search certificate he will take free of any subsequent incumbrances created by the vendor. Any charges which are registered against legal estate owners who held the land before the period covered by the abstracted title will bind a purchaser even though he does not know the names of the estate owners against whom to search. If he suffers loss as a result of these charges he can in certain circumstances claim compensation from the registry.

B. REGISTRATION OF TITLE

1. Purposes

The idea behind the registration of title is to replace the separate investigation of title on every purchase by a title guaranteed by the state. The purchaser inspects the register to see whether the vendor has power to sell the land and what are the most important incumbrances affecting the property. The system is not meant to alter the substantive law but only the conveyancing machinery. However it has become apparent that in many ways there are substantial differences in registered and unregistered land.

2. Classes of interest

In registered land there are three classes of rights: (1) the registered interest i.e. the estate for which a title has been granted by the registrar (2) overriding interests which will bind a purchaser whether he knows of them or not, and (3) minor interests which will only bind a purchaser if protected by some entry on the register.

(a) Registered interests

A legal fee simple and a legal term of years can be registered with a separate title unless in the case of a lease (1) it is for under 21 years or (2) it contains an absolute prohibition against assignment or (3) it is a mortgage.

Various areas in the country are made subject to compulsory registration by statutory instruments. It is hoped that by 1985 all land in England will be subject to compulsory registration.

An application for registration of a freehold title must be made within two months of the first conveyance on sale after the area has become a compulsory registration area.

Whether or not the freehold is registered, when an area has become a compulsory registration area application for registration of the leasehold title must be made within two months after: (a) the first grant of a lease for 40 years or more or (b) the first assignment on sale of an existing lease having at least 40 years to run. Even in a non-compulsory area, if a freehold or leasehold title is registered and the registered proprietor grants a lease for over 21 years the lease must be registered with a separate title in order to confer a legal estate. No time limit applies.

Voluntary registration in a non-compulsory area has been suspended save in exceptional cases, e.g., where deeds have been destroyed or lost, or where there are building estates with more than 20 plots.

(b) Overriding interests

Overriding interests bind a proprietor of registered land even though they are not mentioned on the register and he has no notice of them.

The most important of the overriding interests are legal easements, rights being acquired by adverse possession under the Limitation Act, 1980, local land charges until protected on the register, leases not exceeding 21 years granted at a rent without a premium being taken, and in the case of possessory qualified or good leasehold title all interests excepted from the effect of registration. The category of overriding interests which has caused the most difficulty is, 'the rights of every person in actual occupation of the land or in receipt of the rents and profits thereof, save where enquiry is made of such person and the rights are not disclosed'.

This category would include tenants and those who go into occupation under a mere agreement for a lease. An option to purchase the reversion granted in a lease of registered land will bind a purchaser of the reversion as an overriding interest if the lessee is in occupation even though not protected by a caution or notice on the register. In unregistered land such an option would be void against a purchaser of the reversion if it were not registered as an estate contract.

Rights under a licence have not traditionally been protected as overriding interests. However now that licences by estoppel and some contractual licences are binding on third parties it is difficult to see how such rights in favour of an occupier will not be protected as overriding interests.

If a beneficiary under a bare trust or trust for sale is in occupation his rights will be protected.

HODGSON v. MARKS [1971] Ch 892

An old lady Mrs. Hodgson had a lodger Evans. He told her to transfer the legal estate of her house to him assuring her it would not affect her right in the property, but it would merely make it easier for him to manage the property for her. A purchaser took a transfer of the property from Evans. It was *held* that although he did not know of Mrs. Hodgson's interest, nevertheless because she was in occupation and was entitled to the whole equitable interest which Evans was holding on trust for her, the purchaser was bound by her interest.

WILLIAMS AND GLYN BANK LTD. v. BOLAND [1980] 3 WLR 138

The husband had the legal estate, being the sole registered proprietor. However as the wife had made a contribution to the purchase money the husband was a trustee holding the property for himself and his wife. The husband raised a loan for business purposes secured by a charge on the house in favour of the plaintiff bank. The husband defaulted in the mortgage repayments and the bank sought possession. The bank failed. It was *held* that the wife was in occupation and her right as a benefic-iary under a trust for sale was therefore protected.

It should be noted that rights of beneficiaries under a strict settlement can by statute only exist as minor interests not as overriding interests. Similarly the rights of spouses under the Matrimonial Homes Act, 1967 are specifically excluded from the category of overriding interests.

(c) Minor interests

Minor interests need to be protected by an entry on the register if they are to bind a purchaser. If they are not so protected they will not bind a purchaser whether he knows of them or not.

There are two main categories of minor interests,
(i) Equitable interests of beneficiaries under a settlement or trust for sale. Restrictions on the register will ensure that a purchaser pays the money to two trustees. The interests are then overreached and are no concern of a purchaser.
(ii) Interests, which in unregistered land would need to be protected by registration under the Land Charges Act if they are to bind a purchaser.

Similar protection is given by the Land Registration Act if such interests are protected by an entry on the Land Register. Interests can be protected by:

(i) Notices. A notice ensures that the registered proprietor and anyone deal-ing with the land will take subject to the right protected by the notice. Rights which can be protected by notice include all matters which could be land charges under the Land Charges Act, 1972 including a spouse's right to occupy a house where the other spouse is the registered proprietor. This right as we have seen is specifically excluded from the category of over-riding interests by the Matrimonial Homes Act, 1967.

The Land Certificate must be produced to the Registrar before a notice can be entered on the register. Unless the land certificate is already on deposit at the Land Registry, as it is when there is a charge on the property, the co-operation of the registered proprietor is necessary.

(2) Cautions. There are two kinds of cautions: (i) a caution against first registration. Any person interested in the land may lodge a caution. The Registrar must then inform the cautioner of any application for the registration of title; (ii) a caution against dealing. This protects minor interests where the registered proprietor is unco-operative and will not lodge his Land Certificate. The Registrar must then give notice to the cautioner before any dealing with the land. In both cases the cautioner has a fixed time, usually 14 days, after receiving notice to make his objections known. If he does not object, the caution will be removed. Cautions can protect such interests as options to purchase, equitable charges and easements, but a caution is much less satisfactory than a land charge in unregistered land under the Land Charges Act both because it is subject to the warning off procedure and because the registrar has substantial discretionary powers. He is unwilling to allow cautions to be prolonged indefinitely. Clear titles are favoured at the expense of third party rights.

(3) Inhibitions. These are orders of the court or Registrar which forbid any dealing with the property either absolutely or until a certain time or event. They are only used where there is no other way of protecting a claim, e.g., bankruptcy inhibition will prevent a registered proprietor from disposing of the land.

(4) Restrictions. These are entries made either by the registered proprietor himself or with his consent. They prevent any dealing with the land until some condition has been complied with, e.g., where the registered proprietor is a tenant for life there will probably be restrictions prohibiting the registration of a disposition unless (i) it is authorised by the Settled Land Act and (ii) capital money is paid to at least two trustees.

The position of a lessee with a lease for under 40 years where the lessor's title is registered illustrates clearly the different interests in registered land. e.g.,

(a) A lease for 30 years. As the superior title is registered then the 30 year lease is a registrable interest and must be registered with a separate title in order to confer a legal estate.

(b) A lease for 15 years at a rent without a premium. This cannot be registered with a separate title but being for a term of under 21 years without a fine is an overriding interest.

(c) A lease for 15 years at a rent but a premium has also been paid. This is not an overriding interest as a premium has been paid but only a minor interest. It must be protected by an entry on the register of the landlord's title.

(d) A lease for 15 years at a rent and a premium has been paid but in addition the lessee is in occupation. If the lessee does not protect his lease as a minor interest, it will still be protected as an overriding interest as he is in occupation.

3. Parts of the register

The register is in three parts which are kept together in the District Land Registry. A copy of the entries is contained in the Land Certificate which is given to each registered proprietor.

(a) The property register describes the registered land, refers to the general map or filed plan and contains notes of interests held for the benefit of the land, e.g., easements and restrictive covenants.

(b) The proprietorship register gives the nature of the title (absolute, qualified, possessory or good leasehold). The classification depends on the approval of the registrar. The name, address and description of the proprietor is also set out as with any cautions, inhibitions or restrictions affecting his right to deal with the land.

(c) The charges register contains entries relating to rights adverse to the land, mortgages, restrictive covenants and all notices protecting rights over land.

4. Types of title

(a) Freehold

(i) **Absolute.** The registration of any person as first proprietor with absolute title to freehold vests in that person the legal estate subject to (1) incumbrances and other entries appearing on the register (2) overriding interests (3) where the registered proprietor is not holding for his own benefit (e.g. a trustee) he holds subject to minor interests (e.g. equitable interests of beneficiaries) of which he has notice.

Although absolute title is the best title known to English law it is still only relative. Overriding interests as has been shown can be a major blot on the title. Moreover in certain circumstances the register may be rectified.

(ii) **Possessory.** This has the same effect as absolute title except that registration does not prejudice the enforcement of any adverse interest subsisting at the date of first registration i.e., no guarantee is given in respect of the prior title before the date of first registration.

(iii) **Qualified.** This too has the same effect as absolute except that the property is held subject to some defect or right specified on the register. It is very rare in practice to find a qualified title.

(b) Leasehold

Leasehold titles can be absolute, qualified or possessory in the same way as freehold titles. Lessees will also take subject to the express and implied terms of the lease. Absolute title will only be registered where the freehold and any intermediate leasehold titles have been registered. Absolute leasehold title is a guarantee that (i) the proprietor is owner of the lease and (ii) the lease has been validly granted.

If the freehold and intermediate leasehold titles are not registered then only good leasehold title will be registered. This has the same effect as absolute title but it does not prejudice the enforcement of any interest affecting or in derogation of the title of the lessor to grant the lease, i.e., it does not say that the lease was validly granted. Where the superior title is registered but the lessee only has good leasehold title, even though he is not entitled to inspect the register of such superior title, he will take subject to all entries which appear thereon.

(c) Upgrading of title

As the aim behind the legislation is to facilitate the transfer of a good title, power is given to the registrar to upgrade the category of the title. The Land Registration Act, 1925, provides for the conversion from possessory, qualified or good leasehold to absolute title. If the registrar is satisfied as to possession he is bound to convert the title (i) to absolute in the case of a freehold registered with possessory title for 15 years and (ii) to good leasehold in the case of a leasehold registered with possessory title for 10 years. The registrar has a discretionary right to convert the title (i) to absolute or good leasehold if the land is registered with qualified, possessory or good leasehold title and is transferred for value and (ii) to absolute if the land has been registered with good leasehold title for 10 years and he is satisfied that the owners of the lease have been in possession for that long.

5. Searches

Searches are made against the title number of the property. Where the title is absolute no search is made in the Land Charges Registry which only relates to unregistered land. A search is made for any entries against the title number since the issue of office copy entries, by the Land Registry or the date of the last search, or the last time the Land Certificate was lodged at the Land Registry for official comparison with the register.

Unlike the Land Charges Registry the Land Registry is not open to the public. The authority of the registered proprietor is needed before a search can be made. Besides revealing the up to date entries on the register the search certificate will give the purchaser priority. Provided he lodges his application for registration of the transfer to him within 30 days of such search any registration made during that time will be postponed.

For example: B receives a clear search against A's title number on 1st October. On 5th October A charges the property. On 10th October B lodges his application at the Land Registry. The charge will be postponed.

However, the application must be (a) in order (b) delivered within 30 days (c) sent to the correct District Land Registry. Unlike a Land Charges Search the result of a Land Registry search is not conclusive in favour of a purchaser.

PARKASH v. IRANI FINANCE LTD. [1970] Ch 101

The official search failed to reveal the existence of a caution which had been duly lodged. The cautioner retained priority notwithstanding the ignorance of the purchaser.

6. Rectification

Even where a proprietor has been registered with an absolute title the register may be rectified against him. The Land Registration Act, 1925, s 82 sets out the cases when this may occur, e.g. to enable a person's name to be removed where the entry was made by fraud, where two or more people by mistake are registered as proprietors of the same estate, or where there are errors, omissions or mistakes and it would be just to rectify. However, by section 82(3) the register will not be rectified against a registered proprietor in possession unless (i) it is to give effect to an overriding interest, (ii) such a proprietor has caused or substantially contributed to the error by fraud or lack of proper care or (iii) for any reason it would be unjust not to rectify against him.

Though an applicant is able to bring himself within one of the exceptions to section 82(3) and so claim rectification against a registered proprietor in possession the jurisdiction is discretionary. In assessing justice the court can take into account the fact that rectification would entitle the losing party to indemnity while non-rectification would not. Rectification may still be refused if the indemnity will not be adequate compensation for the loss of the land.

7. Indemnity

The Land Registration Act, 1925, s 83 gives a right to indemnity to persons suffering loss where (i) the register is rectified (ii) the register is not rectified but there is an error or omission (iii) documents lodged at the registry are lost or destroyed or there is an error in an official certificate of search (iv) rectification affects a proprietor claiming in good faith under a forged disposition.

Indemnity for non-rectification is limited to the value of the lost interest at the time when the mistake was made, and will generally be statute-barred under the Limitation Act, 1980 six years after registration. Where the register is rectified the indemnity will be the value of the lost interest immediately before the time of rectification, i.e. the market value.

No indemnity will be paid where the applicant has caused or substantially contributed to the loss by fraud or lack of proper care. Further, there must be loss so no indemnity will be given where rectification is to give effect to an overriding interest. A purchaser takes subject to overriding interests and rectification is only recognising the existing position.

It is often said that under the system of registration the state guarantees the title. This is an exaggerated claim. A transferee always takes subject to overriding interests even though not mentioned on the register. The court has a wide discretion to rectify the register as may seem just, and there are a number of cases where the true owner or innocent purchaser may be left without property or compensation.

12 Contract and Conveyance

OUTLINE

A. Precontract

1. Draft contract
2. Survey
3. Preliminary enquiries
4. Local land charges search and enquiries

B. Formation of Contract

1. Formal contracts
2. Informal contracts

C. Effect of Contract

1. Remedies
2. Position of purchaser
3. Position of vendor
4. Position of 3rd parties

D. Post-contract Conveyancing

1. Title
2. Requisitions
3. Conveyance or transfer
4. Searches
5. Completion
6. Stamping
7. Registration

INTRODUCTION

Conveyancing is the transfer of the legal estate i.e. the fee simple absolute in possession or the term of years absolute, from one party to another. It is a two stage process; first there is a contract then there is a conveyance.

A. PRE-CONTRACT

Often a vendor will find a purchaser through an estate agent. The vendor will agree to sell his property to the purchaser 'subject to contract'. Contracts for the sale of land are governed by the ordinary rules of contract but in addition, to be enforceable by action, must be evidenced in writing. The normal procedure is for the vendor's solicitors to draft a contract using a form with general conditions already printed on it. These conditions can be modified or extended by special conditions to meet the particular circumstances of the case. This form together with a copy is sent to the purchaser's solicitors.

Before entering into a contract the purchaser should make sure that he receives a firm offer of a mortgage. The building society will employ a surveyor to check that the property is an adequate security for the loan. In most cases a building society's surveyor owes no duty of care to the purchaser. The purchaser should employ his own surveyor who should inspect the property for physical defects. The purchaser also should inspect the property and where persons other than the vendor are in occupation of the property ascertain whether they claim any rights.

The ordinary rule of *caveat emptor* (let the buyer beware) applies to contracts for the sale of land. Thus it is up to the purchaser to make searches and enquiries. Against this however the vendor is under a duty to describe the property and estate being sold accurately and he must not make any misrepresentation. He must also disclose latent defects in title, such as restrictive covenants which would not be apparent to a purchaser inspecting the property.

The purchaser's solicitor should make preliminary enquiries of the vendor about the property e.g. the use of the property under the Town and Country Planning Acts, 1947-71, details of subsisting tenancies, easements, observance of restrictive covenants. Normally standard forms are used but a purchaser should ask additional questions where appropriate which are relevant to the property. The vendor's solicitor should reply to these questions after confirming with the vendor that the answers are correct.

The purchaser's solicitor should also make a search in the Register of Local Land Charges maintained by the local authority. This should reveal any orders or notices under various statutes e.g. the Town and Country Planning Acts, 1947-71, Public Health Acts, 1875-1936 and Clean Air Act, 1961. Any charge which is omitted from the search or has not been properly registered will bind a purchaser but he will be entitled to compensation under section 10 of the Local Land Charges Act, 1975. Enquiries should also be made of the local authority concerning matters relating to highways, proposed development, sewers etc.

The solicitor should discuss all these documents and the replies he receives with the purchaser. He should explain to him any special conditions in the contract. It is at this stage that the contract can be amended. The vendor and purchaser are not in a legally binding relationship. Either party is free to break off the negotiations at any time without incurring liability. Thus if the vendor receives a higher offer from another purchaser he is entitled to enter into a new contract. The original purchaser has no redress even if he has incurred the expense of employing a surveyor.

B. THE FORMATION OF THE CONTRACT

Formal contracts

In a normal conveyancing transaction the contract is engrossed in two parts and is not effective until they have been exchanged. The two parts must be identical. The purchaser sends off his part signed and in return the vendor posts his signed part. It is unsettled, in the absence of a condition in the contract covering the position, whether exchange takes place on the posting or receipt of the second part. It has been suggested that because of the complexity of contracts for the sale of land that it should be on the receipt of the second part as the parties would then have the documents with all the terms in front of them. The normal contractual rule is that the contract is formed on the posting of the acceptance. In order to achieve simultaneous exchanges in a chain of transactions solicitors now often effect exchange by telephone.

Informal contracts

Informal contracts can arise where the parties decide not to bother with a formal contract, or where they enter into a contract without realising it, or the exchange procedure falls down and one party wishes to hold the other to the agreement. This is a frequent problem with rising house prices and consequent gazumping.

All that is necessary is that there should be a concluded agreement, which is evidenced in writing and signed by the person against whom the contract is to be enforced. The signed memorandum must contain details of the parties or means of identifying them, the property, the price or a method of ascertaining it and any other agreed terms. A memorandum of a contract for the grant of a lease must also state the commencement and length of the term. Some terms if not express will be implied by law.

To make sure that an enforceable contract is not entered into unintentionally the parties should make sure that any letter they write records that the sale or the purchase is 'subject to contract'. Otherwise they may find that the letter constitutes a sufficient memorandum.

A memorandum is not required where there is a concluded agreement evidenced by a sufficient act of part performance e.g. a person in reliance upon the contract has acted to his detriment by giving up secure accommodation to enter into possession of the property which is the subject of the contract.

C. EFFECT OF THE CONTRACT

The parties are in a legally binding relationship. Remedies are available for breach of contract and misrepresentation. These include rescission of the contract, damages, and an order for specific performance of the contract.

A term is generally included in a contract that a 10% deposit shall be paid on exchange. It is both a part payment of the purchase price and security for the performance of the contract. If the purchaser defaults after the exchange of contracts the vendor can keep the deposit. If an estate agent or solicitor receives the deposit as vendor's agent then the vendor can call for the money and use it for his own purchase. If however the deposit is held by the agent or solicitor as stakeholder he cannot part with the money unless he has the authority of both vendor and purchaser. Should the agent holding a post-contract deposit, either as vendor's agent or stakeholder, default it is the vendor who must bear the loss.

Position of the purchaser

The beneficial ownership passes to the purchaser who is entitled to all the capital gains in value of the property, but must bear all the losses unless they are due to a breach of the vendor's duties. Thus if the property is burnt down the purchaser is still bound to complete. As the risk passes to the purchaser he should insure the property.

Position of the vendor

The vendor retains the legal estate and by the doctrine of conversion is deemed from the date of the contract to have an interest in the proceeds of sale, the purchaser being deemed to have an interest in land. The vendor is entitled to retain possession of the property. He is also entitled to any rents and profits, less outgoings until the contractual date of completion.

The vendor must act in a trustee-like manner, keeping the property in good repair, cultivating the garden and not allowing the property to be damaged. The vendor is not entitled to any indemnity for the cost of any improvements or repairs he makes. The vendor should remove fittings (unless they are included in the contract) but leave fixtures on the property.

Although the vendor is described as a trustee, he is only a qualified trustee. Normally trustees are not entitled to possession or rents and profits but are indemnified for their expenditure. Moreover the vendor's position as trustee depends on the contract being specifically enforceable. Should the contract never be completed the vendor will not be liable for breach of his duty to maintain the property.

Position of third parties

A contract, being an interest in land, is registrable under the Land Charges Act, 1972 as an estate contract. If so registered it will bind a purchaser of the legal estate for money or money's worth. It is not usual however for a purchaser to bother to register an estate contract unless completion is to take place a long time in the future or there are other exceptional circumstances.

D. POST-CONTRACT CONVEYANCING

It is the vendor's duty to show he has a good title to the land. He does not however want to hand over the deeds until he receives the purchase money. Nor does the purchaser want to hand over the money until he has had an opportunity of studying the title. The vendor traditionally supplied the purchaser with an abstract. This gave the material contents of all documents. Preparing an abstract is a skilled and technical job. It involves using different margins strange abbreviations, and converting the words used in deeds to the past and passive tenses. Today it is more usual for the vendor to supply copy documents.

Where the title to land is registered instead of an abstract the vendor should supply the purchaser with office copies of entries on the register and of any filed plans. It is usual for the vendor to supply these before contracts are exchanged. They are obtained from the Land Registry on payment of a small fee. The vendor should also give the purchaser a written authority to inspect the register. The purchaser is entitled to an abstract and evidence if any, on matters on which the register is not conclusive.

Having studied the abstract or office copy entries the purchaser can raise requisitions on title. The vendor is bound to answer all questions relevant to the abstracted title.

Subject to receiving satisfactory replies to his requisitions the purchaser's solicitor drafts the conveyance. This should contain an up to date description of the property. It should be sent with a copy to the vendor's solicitors for approval or amendment. An engrossed conveyance is prepared by the purchaser's solicitor and sent to the vendor's solicitor for execution by his client.

In registered land the purchaser will provide a draft transfer rather than a conveyance. Numerous forms are available and can be simply filled in with additions if necessary. A purchaser after being satisfied with the replies to his requisitions will usually suggest that the vendor treats the top copy as an engrossment.

Shortly before completion a purchaser should make his searches. In unregistered land he should search in the Land Charges Register against the vendor and against all previous owners of the legal estate in the period covered by the abstract of title except against those for whom there are produced earlier satisfactory official certificates of search. The result of the search is conclusive in favour of a purchaser and will give him protection against a last minute registration. Thus if completion takes place within 15 working days after the result of the official certificate the purchaser is not affected by any entry made on the register after the date of the certificate and before completion.

If the land is registered a search should be made accompanied by the authority to inspect the register, in the Land Registry against the title number of the property being bought. The search covers the period to the date of the search from either the issue of the office copy entries or the date of the last search or the date when the Land Certificate was last lodged at the Land Registry for official comparison with the register. The search is not conclusive but the purchaser who receives an incorrect reply to his search is entitled to compensation.

Any entry made after the date of an official certificate of search will be postponed to the purchaser's transfer provided he lodges his application for registration within 30 days of the result of his search. The application must be in order and delivered to the appropriate district land registry. There is an extension procedure if the application cannot be lodged within the permitted time.

Completion

Completion occurs when the purchaser pays the purchase price in return for the delivery of the conveyance or transfer. This normally takes place at the offices of the vendor or his mortgagee, though it is possible to complete by post.

The task of the vendor

The vendor's solicitor has to receive the purchase money, either in the form of a bankers draft or in cash. He should not accept a cheque without his client's authority as, if it bounces, he would be liable for the loss. If the deposit has been paid to a third party e.g. estate agent as stakeholder, he will need a letter from the purchaser authorising such deposit to be released.

The vendor must produce the deeds for inspection by the purchaser. The vendor should hand over to the purchaser the conveyance to him and the title deeds as listed on a schedule, a copy of which, signed by the purchaser, should be retained by the vendor. If the title is registered then the vendor should give the purchaser the transfer to him and the Land Certificate. There may also be other relevant documents a vendor should hand over e.g. a licence to assign, lease, National House Building Council Certificate.

Where there is a mortgage to be discharged completion will generally take place at the mortgagee's solicitor's offices. A draft will be paid to the mortgagee and a second draft for the balance of the purchase price to the vendor. The mortgagee will have the deeds and hand them to the purchaser including a deed of discharge or vacating receipt on the mortgage. In the case of a Building Society an undertaking is usually given to discharge the mortgage and forward it to the purchaser within a certain number of days.

Shortly before completion the vendors will have sent a completion statement to the purchaser setting out the monies due including any apportionments of general and water rates and rent where applicable. Receipts must be produced by the vendor to evidence that payments have been made to the dates set out on the completion statement.

There may be miscellaneous matters for the vendor to attend to e.g. an authority to an agent to release the keys to the purchaser, or to tenants to pay future rents to the new landlord. If there are any outstanding matters the vendor's solicitor may give undertakings to attend to them.

The task of the purchaser

The purchaser should examine the title deeds against the abstract already supplied to him. He should collect the deeds which are to be handed over and in cases where the deeds are retained by the vendor make sure that an endorsment is made noting the conveyance or, where the title is registered, he should collect the Land Certificate and transfer. He must make sure that any outstanding mortgages are vacated or get an undertaking for their discharge.

He should pay to the vendor the balance of the purchase price and any other monies due. If the deposit is held by a third party as stakeholder, he will need to hand over a release of deposit. Where the purchaser is buying the house with a mortgage the mortgagee will provide a draft for part of the completion monies. In return the mortgagee will collect the deeds, the conveyance or transfer, and a mortgage deed signed by the purchaser.

The purchaser should inspect the receipts for general and water rates and rent where appropriate to ensure that the payments tie up with the figures given in the completion statement.

He should check up on any miscellaneous matters, e.g. keys, licences to assign. If there is anything outstanding he should obtain the undertaking of the vendor's solicitor to attend to it.

The above is a very simple outline of the procedure on completion. Where companies, new houses, leases etc. are concerned there are additional matters which must be dealt with by both vendor and purchaser.

Post-completion

The purchaser, or the mortgagee, must attend to the stamping of the conveyance or transfer. Even if no *ad valorem* stamp duty is payable the document must be marked under the Finance Act, 1931. An instrument which is not duly stamped is not admissible in evidence.

In unregistered land the legal estate passes to the purchaser on delivery of the deed which will normally be deemed to be at completion. In registered land the legal estate only passes on registration of the new proprietor. The purchaser should lodge his application for registration of the transfer within the priority period given him by his search certificate. If this is not possible, an extension procedure is available. Moreover, where a transfer has to be adjudicated for stamp duty the documents can be lodged at the land registry with a request that the transfer should be returned. Priority is thus retained and the transfer can be re-lodged at the land registry after stamping.

Set out below is a diagram summarising the main steps taken in a simple conveyancing transaction. There are no differences in procedure pre-contract in registered land and unregistered land. Post-contract differences exist in deducing title, form of transfer and passing of the legal estate.

PRE-CONTRACT

Vendor's solicitors   **Purchaser's solicitors**

(1) Sends draft contract and copy
    to purchaser

    (2) (i) Reads contract carefully
        (ii) Makes preliminary inquiries with vendor.
      (iii) Inspects property
     (iv) Has Survey
      (v) Makes local land charge search and inquiries

(3) Answers preliminary inquiries

    (4) Returns one copy draft contract approved or amended

    (5) Purchasers' signed copy sent with 10 per cent deposit to vendor's solicitor.

(6) Vendor's signed copy sent to purchaser on receipt of purchaser's part.

EFFECT

The vendor and purchaser are in a legally binding relationship. The vendor is a qualified trustee for the purchaser. The beneficial ownership passes to the purchaser. He should insure.

POST-CONTRACT

Vendor's solicitor

(7) Vendor supplies title to purchaser
  (a) Unregistered land: abstract (or epitome of title with copy documents) tracing legal estate from a deed at least 15 years old until it vests in vendor.
  (b) Registered land:
    (i) Copy entries of the register and any filed plan
    (ii) Authority to inspect the register
   (iii) Abstract and evidence on matters on which register not conclusive

Purchaser's solicitor

    (8) Raises requisitions on title

(9) Answers requisitions

(10) Sends draft conveyance if unregistered, or draft transfer if registered, to vendor.

(11) Approves or amends draft conveyance or transfer

(12) Engrosses deed and sends to vendor

(13) Vendor executes conveyance or transfer

(14) Searches
    (i) Unregistered land
    Land Charge search against estate owners who held land during period covered by the abstract (unless previous search certificates produced)
    (ii) Registered land
    Land Registry search against title number.

(15) Completion. Collects draft and letter authorising release of deposit.

(15) Completion
    (i) Unregistered land. Checks deeds against abstract, collect deeds, conveyance
    (ii) Registered
    Checks and collects land certificate and transfer

(16) Stamps conveyance or transfer

(17) Registered land
Lodges application for registration of transfer.

Index to Statutes

Administration of Justice Act, 1970, 82
Agricultural Holdings Act, 1948, 46

Building Societies Act, 1962, 81

Civil Aviation Act, 1949, 5
Clean Air Act, 1961, 98
Coal Industry (Nationalisation) Act, 5

Finance Act, 1931, 103

Housing Act, 1957, 64

Land Charges Act, 1972, 11, 38, 56, 67,
   81, 82, 85, 86, 89, 100
Land Registration Act, 1925, 12, 82,
   83-94
   s 82, 93
   s 83, 93
Landlord and Tenant Act, Part II, 1954,
   46
Law of Property Act, 1925, 22, 24, 39
   s 1, 9
   s 30, 22
   s 36, 27, 31
   s 40, 38, 77
   s 56, 61
   s 62, 71
   s 78, 63
   s 79, 63
   s 84, 64
   s 141, 45

Law of Property (Joint Tenants) Act,
   1964, 33
Leasehold Property Repairs Act, 1938,
   41
Leasehold Reform Act, 1967, 49, 62

Matrimonial Homes Act, 1967, 86, 89

National Parks and Access to the
   Countryside Act, 1949, 68

Petroleum (Production) Act, 1934, 5
Prescription Act, 1832, 72
Public Health Acts, 1875-1936, 98

Right of Light Act, 1959, 72

Settled Land Act, 1925, 15, 16, 17,
   24
   s 18, 17
   s 19(2), 32
   s 36(1), 32
   s 110, 17
   s 110(5), 18, 24
Supreme Court of Judicature Act, 1873,
   54

Town and Country Planning Act, 1971,
   5, 61, 97, 98

Water Resources Act, 1963, 5

Index to Cases

Allen v. Greenwood, 73

Bernstein v. Skyview Gardens Ltd, 5
Binions v. Evans, 54
Bradley v. Carritt, 79
Re Buchanan-Wollaston's Conveyance,
   22
Bull v. Bull, 32
Burgess v. Rawnsley, 31

Caunce v. Caunce, 33
Cityland and Property (Holdings) Ltd
   v. Dabrath, 79
Crabb v. Arun District Council, 56
Cuckmere Brick Co. Ltd v. Mutual
   Finance Ltd, 81

D'Eyncourt v. Gregory, 3

Elliston v. Reacher, 64
E.R. Ives Investments Ltd v. High, 53
Errington v. Errington, 54
Esso Petroleum v. Harpers Garage
   (Stourport) Ltd, 80

Fairclough v. Swan Brewery Co. Ltd, 98
Federated Homes Ltd v. Mill Lodge
   Properties Ltd, 63

Halsall v. Brizell, 62
Hill v. Tupper, 67
Hodgson v. Marks, 68

Inwards v. Baker, 59

Jones v. Challenger, 22

Re Kempthorn, 23
Knightsbridge Estate Trusts Ltd v.
   Byrne, 78
Kreglinger v. New Patagonia Meat and
   Cold Storage Co. Ltd., 79

Leigh v. Taylor, 3

Re Morgan's Lease, 17
Moule v. Garrett, 44

Noakes and Co. Ltd v. Rice, 79

Parkash v. Irani Finance Ltd., 93
Pascoe v. Turner, 56
Pereira v. Vandiyar, 42
Phipps v. Pears, 68

Tanner v. Tanner, 53
Tulk v. Moxhay, 62

Wheeldon v. Burrows, 70, 71
White v. City of London Brewery Co.,
   81
Williams v. Glyn Ltd. v. Boland, 89
Wong v. Beaumont Property Trust Ltd,
   70
Wood v. Leadbitter, 54

108

General Index

agricultural holdings, 46
air space, 5
assent, 16
assignment
    lease, 44
    restrictive covenant in equity, 63

bankruptcy of tenant, 41
benefit and burden, 55, 56

charge by way of legal mortgage, 9
completion, 101, 102
conditional fee, 10, 12, 15
conditions of sale, 97
constructive notice, 11
contracts for the sale of land, 38, 97,
    98, 99
conversion doctrine of, 23, 100
conveyance, 101, 102, 103, 104, 105
co-ownership, 27-34
    determination, 33
    joint tenancy, 29, 30, 31
    joint tenants for life, 32
    severance, 30, 31
    tenancy in common, 32
        equitable presumptions, 30
    trust for sale statutory, 21
    trustees, 22
    undivided shares, 30
    union, 33
    unities of joint tenants, 29
covenants
    building scheme, 64
    discharge, 64
    indemnity, 44, 62
    in leases, 42, 43, 44, 45
    restrictive covenants, 10, 59-64
curtain principle, 16, 22

deposit, 99
derogation from grant, 42, 69
determinable fee, 10, 15

easements, 67-73
    acquisition, 69, 70, 71
    conditions, 67, 68
    continuous and apparent, 71
    equitable, 10, 11, 67
    express grant, 70
    extent of, 73
    extinguishment, 73
    implied grant of, 70, 71, 72
    intended easements, 70, 71
    legal interests, 67
    light rights of, 72
    natural rights, 68
    necessity, 70
    prescription, 71-72
        common law, 71
        lost modern grant, 71
        statutory, 71, 72
    release, 73
    reservation, 73
    support, 68
    way rights of, 73
equity
    equitable easement, 10, 11, 67,
        86
    equitable estoppel, 11, 55, 56
    equitable interest, 10, 11
    equitable lease, 10, 38
    equitable mortgage, 77
    equity of redemption, 78, 79,
        80
estate, 9, 12
estate contracts, 10, 38, 100

fee simple, 9
fee tail, 10, 15
fixtures, 3, 100
freehold estate, 9

infants, 15

joint tenancy, 29, 30, 31

land definition, 3
land charges
landlord and tenant, 35-49
leaseholds, 4, 35-49
  assignments, 37
  covenants in leases, 42-43
  derogation from grant, 47
  enfranchisement, 48, 49, 62
  enlargement of lease, 62
  equitable lease, 10, 38
  essentials of lease, 37, 38
  fixed term lease, 38
  forfeiture, 40
    bankruptcy of tenant, 40, 41
    breaches of covenant, 40, 41
    non-payment of rent, 40, 41
    relief against, 40, 41
    subtenants, 41
    waiver, 40
  formalities, 38
  future leases, 38
  leases for lives, 39
  legal estate, 9
  merger, 40
  notice to quit, 40
  obligations of landlord and tenant,
    42, 43
  option to purchase reversion, 43, 44,
    48
  periodic tenancies, 9, 38
  perpetually renewable leases, 39, 40
  quiet enjoyment covenant from, 42
  registered land, 90
  rent restriction, 46-49
  repair, 43
  security of tenure, 46-49
    agricultural holdings, 46
    business premises, 46, 47
    enfranchisement, 48
    long tenancies, 48
    protected tenancies, 47, 48
    regulated tenancy, 47, 48
    resident landlord, 47, 48
    restricted contract, 48
    statutory tenancy, 47, 48
  sub-lease, 45
  surrender of lease, 40
  tenancy at sufferance, 39
  termination of leases, 40, 41
  usual covenants, 42
  waste, 43
  year tenancy, 39
legal charge, 9, 77
legal estate, 9, 16, 21, 24
licences, 10
  bare, 53

  contractual, 53, 54
  coupled with an interest, 53
  equitable, 11, 55, 56
life estate, 10, 12, 16, 21
local land charges, 98

matrimonial home, 86, 89
mortgages, 33, 77-82
  by demise, 77
  collateral advantages, 78
  deposit of title deeds, 77
  discharge of, 82
  equitable, 10, 77, 86
  equity of redemption, 78, 79, 80
  foreclosure, 80
  legal charge, 77, 90
  mortgagee
    liability of, 81
    remedies of, 80, 81
  possession mortgagee's right to, 81
  postponement of redemption, 78
  puisne mortgage, 85
  receiver, mortgagee's power to
    appoint, 81
  redemption, 78
  registration, 85, 86, 91
  sale mortgagee's power of, 81

notice, doctrine of, 11

option to purchase, 44, 88
overreaching, 11, 17, 18, 23, 33

part performance, doctrine of, 38, 99
personal property, 3, 4
personal representatives
  special, 32
planning permission, 4, 5
preliminary enquiries, 97
prescription, 71, 72
privity of estate, 44, 45
profits, 69
purchaser, 7, 11, 13, 17, 18, 19, 23, 24,
  28, 33, 97, *etseq*
public rights, 68

real property, 3
re-entry, 11
registered conveyancing, 100-105
registration of charges, 11
  local land charges, 98
  searches, 92, 101
registration of title, 87-94
  cautions, 90
  compulsory, 87
  dispositions of registered land, 87

indemnity, 93, 94
inhibitions, 90
land certificate, 91
leases, 90
minor interests, 89
notices, 89
overriding interests, 88
rectification, 93
register parts of, 91
registered interests, 87
restrictions, 90
titles nature and conversion, 91, 92
voluntary, 88
remainder, 15
rentcharge, 9, 10
requisitions, 100, 101
restrictive covenants, 10, 61-64, 86
reversion, 15, 37, 44, 45

searches
unregistered land, 86, 101
registered land, 92, 101
security of tenure, 45-48
settlements, 13
compared with trusts for sale, 24, 25
curtain principle, 16
discharge died of, 18
duration, 18
improvements, 16
infancy of tenant for life, 16
leases, 17
overreaching, 11, 17, 18
settled land, 13-18
statutory owner, 16

tenant for life, 16
as trustee, 16, 17
powers, 16
trust instrument, 16
trustees of settlement, 17
vesting instrument, 16
stamping, 103
survey, 97

tenancies, 37-49
tenancy in common, 32
tenant for life, 16
term of years, 9, 37-49
title, 100, 101
treasure trove, 5
trusts for sale, 19-25
compared with strict settlements, 24, 25
consents to sale, 22
co-ownership, 21, 27-34
curtain principle, 22
delegation of powers, 23
intestacy, 21
overreaching, 23, 33
postponing sale, 22
powers of trustees, 20

undivided shares, 30

vendor, 97 *etseq*
vesting instrument, 16

waste, doctrine of, 16, 43
water rights, 5